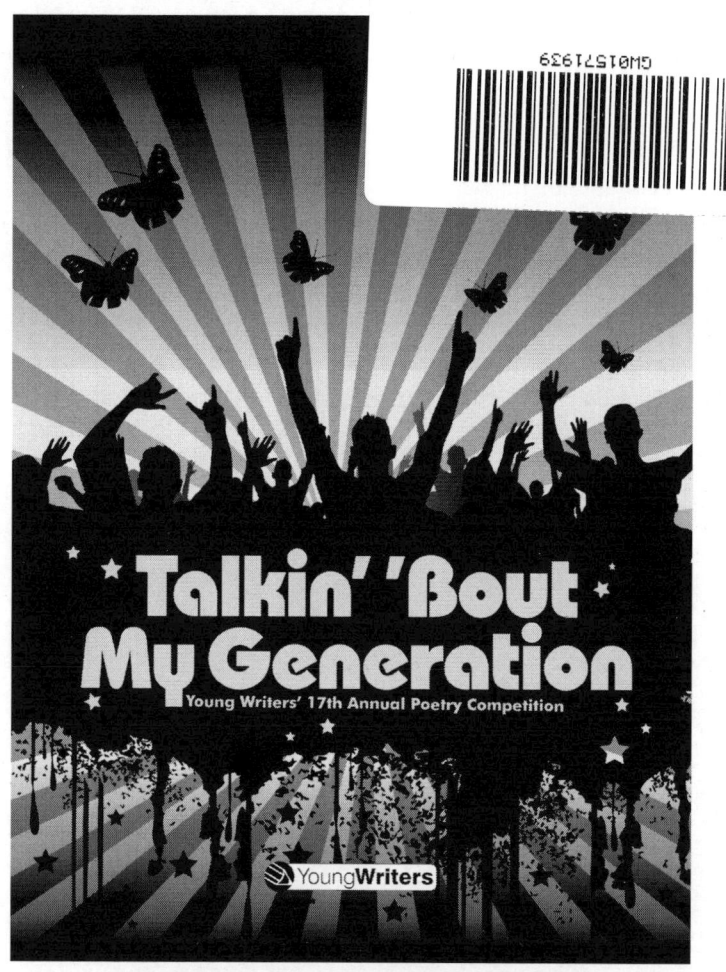

Talkin' 'Bout My Generation

Young Writers' 17th Annual Poetry Competition

South West England

Edited by Michelle Afford

First published in Great Britain in 2008 by:
Young Writers
Remus House
Coltsfoot Drive
Peterborough
PE2 9JX
Telephone: 01733 890066
Website: www.youngwriters.co.uk

All Rights Reserved

© Copyright Contributors 2008

SB ISBN 978-1 84431 698 4

Foreword

This year, the Young Writers' *Talkin' 'Bout My Generation* competition proudly presents a showcase of the best poetic talent selected from thousands of up-and-coming writers nationwide.

Young Writers was established in 1991 to promote the reading and writing of poetry within schools and to the young of today. Our books nurture and inspire confidence in the ability of young writers and provide a snapshot of poems written in schools and at home by budding poets of the future.

The thought, effort, imagination and hard work put into each poem impressed us all and the task of selecting poems was a difficult but nevertheless enjoyable experience.

We hope you are as pleased as we are with the final selection and that you and your family continue to be entertained with *Talkin' 'Bout My Generation South West England* for many years to come.

Contents

Natasha Middleditch (14) — 1

Bristol Cathedral School, Bristol

Connor Chudleigh (12) — 2
Ryan Todd (12) — 2
Connall Lee (13) — 3
Carl Nissen (13) — 3
Tara Williams (12) — 4
Robert Stanfield (13) — 4
Freddie Murray-Browne (13) — 5
Peter Higgins (12) — 5
Aislinn Mooney (13) — 6
Simran Panesar (13) — 7
Isaac Mehraj (12) — 8
Becky Payne (13) — 9
Lawrence Luffman (12) — 10
Andreas Aristotelous (12) — 11
Georgia Wathan (12) — 12
George McCarthy (12) — 13
Huw Grant (12) — 14
Isabella Salisbury (13) — 15
Ross Geddes (12) — 16
Matthew Titcomb (12) — 17
Henry Lodge (13) — 18
Oliver Sullivan (14) — 19
Peter Dixon (13) — 19
Saydee Rumbelow (12) — 20
James Clarke (12) — 21
Hannah Javid (12) — 21
Corin Ward (12) — 22

Chipping Campden School, Chipping Campden

Cameron Craig (12) — 22
Lauren Wright (13) — 23
Catriona Bone (12) — 24

Knowles Hill School, Newton Abbot
 Samantha Boarer (17)   25

Langside Special School, Poole
 Robert Lockwood (18)   26

Mangotsfield Secondary School, Bristol
 Russell Peters (14)   26
 Ty Netherwood (13)   27
 Jasmine Pearce (14)   27
 Kristina Chamberlain (13)   28
 Louis Huxley (13)   28
 Jack Trickey (13)   29
 Charlie Stargatt (13)   29
 Emma English (14)   30
 Dan Hinsley (13)   31
 Amy Joyce (14)   32
 Patrick Dennehy (13)   33
 Joe Weston (13)   34
 Neal Goodman (13)   34
 Oscar Ryan-Reed (14)   35
 Abbey Smart (14)   35
 Claire Fudge (14)   36
 Alex Bryant (14)   37

Newent Community School, Newent
 Tom Berkeley (12)   38

Notton House School, Chippenham
 Michael Barry (15)   39
 Joel Johnson (14)   39

Oldfield School, Bath
 Holly Woodrow (12)   40

Paignton Community & Sports College, Paignton
 Meg Ryan (14)   41
 Katie Cleanthous (18)   42

St Bede's Catholic College, Bristol
  Sam Pembery (12) 43

St Joseph's Catholic College, Swindon
  James Bishop (12) 44
  Michael Fawcett 44
  Cameron Gordon (12) 45
  Alana Turner (15) 45
  Gavin Cowie (12) 46
  Abigail Finneran (15) 47
  Gary Rains 48
  Tim Reuby (14) 49
  Alex Wood 50
  Gabrielle Liddiard (12) 51
  Rebecca Morgan (15) 52
  Rebecca Hooper 53
  Zoe Checchia (15) 54
  Holly Fuller (14) 55
  Sara Conway 56

South Molton Community College, South Molton
  Peter Keighley (14) 57
  Laura Short (14) 58
  Laura Dennis (13) 59
  Kate Carter (13) 60
  Bryony Zeitzen (13) 60
  Cameron Cree (13) 61
  Jack Smith (13) 61
  Louis Hardy (12) 62

The Cotswold School, Cheltenham
  Beth Taylor (13) 62
  Camille Smith (12) 63
  Hannah Davis (14) 64
  Natasha Surch (13) 65
  Lee Salf (14) 66
  Ben Brown (13) 67
  Claire Fisher (13) 68
  Louis Millar (14) 69

Laura Martin (14)   69
Lauren Castleton-White (13)   70
Matt Gibson (13)   71

Torquay Boys' Grammar School, Torquay

Odin Anstiss Liljefors (14)   72
Charlie Hill (12)   73
Matt Carr (14)   75
Tom Charlton (13)   75
Jay Cooper (12)   76
Xennor May (14)   76
Karan Purewal (12)   77
Jack Fletcher (13)   77
Lewis Rowden (14)   78
Michael Curran (14)   78
Johnny Foster (14)   79
Jack Oades (13)   79
Ben Hustwayte (13)   80
Calum Luke (12)   80
Rowan Naidoo (14)   81
Matt Woods (14)   81
Jasper James (13)   82
Yussef Robinson (12)   82
Chris Robson-Close (13)   83
Harry Morse (12)   83
Alistair Roberts (14)   84
Steven Ford (13)   84
Mark Portnoi (14)   85
Henry Lister (13)   85
Tom Owens (13)   86
Iain Tinkler (14)   86
Jake Wilkinson (13)   87
Josh Reilly (12)   87
Lloyd Barwood (13)   88
Luke Breyley (14)   89
Nathan Gilpin (14)   90
Joe Reed (14)   90
James Tucker (12)   91
Phil Reddaway (12)   91

Rob Harris (13)	92
Kieran Hill-Cousins (13)	92
Edward Lovell (13)	93
Henry Booth (11)	93
Dan Ponsford (12)	94
Alex Dyer (11)	94
Daniel Paton (11)	95
Graeme Tinkler (12)	95
Alex Bird (12)	96
William Sambells (12)	96
Joseph Fath (12)	97
Harry Loader (12)	97
Ben Hetherington (11)	98
Tom Godwin (11)	99
Carl Johnson (12)	99
Tom Fullalove (12)	100
Ronan Yeo (11)	101
Kieran Brookes (11)	102

Torquay Grammar School for Girls, Torquay

Kate Rowbottom (12)	103
Bethany Pearce (12)	104
Marina Scholtz (12)	104
Alexandra Searle (11)	105
Daisy Shirley (11)	105
Rebekah Cockram (12)	106
Megan Dorrans (12)	107
Chelsea Mitchell (12)	108
Katie Needham (13)	109
Daisy McArdle & Georgina Watt (13)	110
Bethany Day (12)	111
Emma Singleton (12)	112
Ami Leanna Hardy (12)	113
Hannah Schofield (12)	114
Evie Reed (12)	115
Darcey Roberts (11)	116
Harriet Rowden (12)	116
Sarah Stoyle (12)	117
Emily Attwood Bloomfield (11)	117

Jo Thorpe (11)	118
Rebecca Thorne (12)	119
Teagan Feakins (12)	120
Dani Cole (11)	121
Elizabeth Jones (11)	122
Annabel Strickland (13)	123
Amelia Reid (12)	124
Emily Jepson (12)	124
Charlie Hart (12)	125
Esther Crompton (11)	125
Lauren Grace Harper (11)	126
Laura Harrison (11)	126
Rosalind Gray (12)	127
Kirstie Gibling (11)	127
Laura Powell (12)	128
Eve Parsons (11)	129
Rosie Wood (12)	130
Tiàna May (12)	131
Brittany Brown (11)	132
Helen Gillard (12)	133
Jessica Knapman (11)	134
Brogan Ferrol (11)	135
Tilly Ross (12)	136
Lucy Kember (13)	137
Isabelle Walford (12)	138
Constance Collier-Qureshy (12)	139
Harriet Cox (11)	140
Zoe Gluning (12)	141
Chloe Scott-Perkins (12)	142
Rebecca Squire (12)	143
Sophie Biddick (12)	144
Hayley Norman (12)	145
Emily Watton (12)	146
Emily Plester (12)	147
Demi Butcher (13)	148
Livvy Davidson (12)	148
Sukayna Zayer (12)	149
Chloe Murthwaite (13)	149
Catherine Seymour (13)	150
Philippa Adams (13)	151

Lucy Ricketts (11) — 152
Isabelle Sach (13) — 153
Courtney Beth Clarke (11) — 154
Amy Britton (11) — 155
Emma Pottle (13) — 155
Ashleigh Catherine Rawlings (11) — 156

Truro High School for Girls, Truro

Vicky Hall (13) — 156
Kelly Bowden (13) — 157
Anna Phillips (12) — 157
Jade Bowmer (12) — 158
Tippi Jensen (13) — 158
Lauren Bose (12) — 159
Danielle Blackburn (12) — 159
Katie Slater (13) — 160
Rosie Curry (13) — 161

Twynham School, Christchurch

Amy Mayne (16) & Holly Doick (17) — 162
Elieze Hinchcliffe (11) — 162
William Broomfield (12) — 163
Callum Mercer (12) — 163
Jerome Parramore (12) — 164
Scott Couldridge (14) — 165
Seana Morrison (12) — 166
Danielle Palombo (12) — 166
Ella Somers (12) — 167
Ashley Reedman (12) — 167
Kelly Haynes (11) — 168
Jordan Trellis (11) — 169
Ruby Caitlin McMahon (11) — 170
Georgia Smith & Lauren Fry (14) — 171
Elizabeth Coombes (13) & Katie Mitchell (14) — 172
Holly Du Cros (12) — 172
Sophie Duffell (12) — 173
Georgina Farmer (13) — 173
Amber Porter (11) — 174
Zoë Seabourne (11) — 175

Laura Maw (13)	176
Sarah Bishop (13) & Shannon Vare (14)	177
Emily Rogers (12)	178
Bethany De-Pledge (13)	178
Emily Fardell (13)	179
Hannah McGuigan (12)	179
Alex Burgess (11)	180
Annabel Heybourne (12)	180
Tobias Baril (11)	181
Jack Whitton (11)	182
Sophie Herbert (12)	182
Oliver Shortell (13)	183
Emma Horn (12)	183
Carla Tungate (12)	184
Emma Nunney (12)	185
Charlotte Hubbard (12)	186
Alexandra Wilson (13)	187
Hushai Ian Pineda (12)	188
Hannah Brindley (12)	188
Romy Garner (12)	189

The Poems

No Understanding

Innocent people, missed lives
Forever in our memories from the day they died
Murdered for power
Murdered! No guilt!
Victims of terrorism
With no understanding
Why would they do that?
Why? Cos they're angry?
Angered with jealousy
Jealous to no end
Of what? Is the question we will never comprehend.

The pain they have caused will never go away
The grief, the loss
Thought of every day
How selfish of them
How painful it is
But no one will bring them back
Without them, they'll win!
Win what? A war?
Through fighting, bombing, more?
Power-hungry minds torturing thoughts
Blood, dead bodies
More people dying
Innocent lives lost
Families torn apart
Because . . . of what?

Natasha Middleditch (14)

The Meaning Of Life

There is something you can search and search for
But it never has been found.
It is something to which you are eternally bound
So why would you complete it
When there has never been a point
To your walking on the ground?
And why would you live it
Even though it has always been renowned?
You know what it is
But where is the point?
So, this is the one thing which you must anoint
That when you search for the reason
For all the love and all the treason
You shall live life through every season.

Connor Chudleigh (12)
Bristol Cathedral School, Bristol

The Meaning Of Life

The meaning of life
What is it?
Nobody knows
But what do I think it is?
Is it birth?
Is it charm?
Is it freedom?
Is it harm?

Do I care or shall I carry on wondering
And keep living my life?
I think that's what I'll do
And then, maybe
Just maybe
I'll find the answer
But until then, I'll just wonder.

Ryan Todd (12)
Bristol Cathedral School, Bristol

Power

Power can corrupt even the nicest of people
Power is the cause of a lot of the trouble in the world
If someone has power, they basically do what they want
With money, comes power
Money is the one thing people do anything to get
In some cases, kill people.

But if power did not exist
There would be no rules
And with no rules, people would be robbing other people
Killing themselves and others around them
And generally being evil.

There would be confusion
And this world would be a wreck!

Connall Lee (13)
Bristol Cathedral School, Bristol

The Cheetah

There's a cheetah on the grass,
Going very fast.
Chasing its prey,
Nearly all the day.

It is very hot,
Right in this spot.
The clustering clouds swirling,
On this deadly hot Tuesday.

The cheetah's on the grass,
Going very fast
And a tree is in the way
To the cheetah's dismay,
The cheetah's prey gets away.

Carl Nissen (13)
Bristol Cathedral School, Bristol

Bus Route Stranger

Do you love me?

Do you not?
I can't decide; we've never spoken.

Your aftershave in the morning
Your smile at night.

How could it be you'd ever look
At someone like me?

But this thing I know indeed:
You've taken my heart and touched my life.
The air seems . . . clearer;
The sun feels . . . nearer
And my eyes more open
I see the world for the place that it is.

How could it be that the love
Of someone I may never know could do this?

I owe it all to you
My bus route stranger.

Tara Williams (12)
Bristol Cathedral School, Bristol

Global Warming

When will people understand?
When will people stop?
When will people turn around and put right what is not?
When will people stop polluting?
When will people think?

When will the world realise the small things they can do
Will brighten the future for people like you?

We must all act now, before it's too late
We must all do simple things, like turning off the light
To washing at thirty and turning down the heater at night.

Robert Stanfield (13)
Bristol Cathedral School, Bristol

The Lonely Deer

As the autumn wind blew the leaves,
The trees sighing at their effort,
There walked a lonely deer,
Searching for comfort.
It strode until it found the river,
At which it dipped its head,
Until it heard a noise,
A noise which, to it, said,
'Humans are coming; everyone must run,
Stop what you are doing or you will get shot by a gun.'
So at this, it hurried towards the sun,
But suddenly, it was trapped; it had nowhere to turn.
Humans to the left and humans to the right,
The last thing this deer thought, was about its wife and son.

Freddie Murray-Browne (13)
Bristol Cathedral School, Bristol

My Best Friends

Number one is Lawrence,
Who is kind and thoughtful,
A bit like Kieran,
Who is good at football.
Now onto number three,
Isaac Mehraj,
He is clever and successful
And he supports Arsenal.
Now to Connor, who is funny and cool,
The same with Harry,
Jacob, Ryan and Arran Connell on the guitar
And Rob on the drums
And now to Josh, who is always fun,
A bit like Freddie and Callum,
Oh, what fun!

Peter Higgins (12)
Bristol Cathedral School, Bristol

Writing

Writing has a heartbeat,
The rhythm of the pen.
The speed depends on what's being written,
Who and where and when.

A toddler with a crayon,
Graffiti on the wall.
The woodworm feels the heartbeat,
Vibrations as they crawl.

A grandad with an ink pen
Writes lovingly and slow.
The ageing heartbeat rhythm,
Has a voice so rich and low.

A poet with a pencil,
Writes in the heart of night.
He scribbles down a heartbeat,
As inspiration strikes.

I sit here with a Biro
Writing all alone
And I can feel my heartbeat,
Beating in my poem.

Writing has a heartbeat,
The rhythm of the pen.
It all depends on what was written
Who, where, when.

Aislinn Mooney (13)
Bristol Cathedral School, Bristol

Formula One Poem

There I am, in the car
Ready to accelerate

Waiting, sweating, just . . .
For the light to change

The adrenaline pumping, flowing
Waiting to win the race

I am just there
Doing what I do best

Speeding
Pushing myself to my limits

There's my team
Waiting for me to come into the pits

Just like that, I am off again
Throttling, trying to get a grip of the wheel

Here I am just moments away from victory
Hoping nothing happens

I've crossed the line
Abolished all my opponents

Arriving on the podium
Just getting the trophy
And feeling the champagne going down my face.

Simran Panesar (13)
Bristol Cathedral School, Bristol

My Box
(Inspired by 'Magic Box' by Kit Wright)

My box is very special to me,
That's why I treasure thee.
When I recall what joys we've had,
I always think of our last laugh.

I put in the box . . .

An end to poverty,
Stone soup
And a bonkers, bouncing blue orb.

I put in my box . . .

The eighth wonder of the world,
The solution to climate change
And the last dodo to roam Earth.

My box is made of . . .

Diamonds that were formed millions of years ago,
The swish of a silk sari,
The skin of the snake that bit Cleopatra
And ash from Mount Everest.

I kept my box . . .

In a place unimaginable to Man,
In another world, so no one can retrieve it.

I found my box . . .

Under the Lake District
Which dried up millenniums ago,
I saw it there,
The diamonds were frozen like a ten-thousand-year-old glacier.

The time has come,

For us to go our ways,
I will never forget you, box,
Even when you forget me,
You will be like an unforgettable memory.

Isaac Mehraj (12)
Bristol Cathedral School, Bristol

This Generation

When my head hits my pillow,
A light goes off in my attic.
A whole factory working like clockwork,
Full of thoughts,
Of how I wish the world would be.

The more sensitive signs of: *do not smoke*
For the thought of people who do not read
They decide to pass their fumes to children.

And the: *don't drop litter*
It becomes their world
Rummaging through the plastic bags
Just to feed.

And the brighter things
Of bluer skies
And fluffy clouds.

But now, for reality,
Lying on my pillow,
I wish it were stuffed with feathers.

Becky Payne (13)
Bristol Cathedral School, Bristol

The Meaning Of Life

What is the meaning of life?
I've heard many people ask me that question,
Why we are not told
No one knows
Does anyone care?
Maybe we are told,
When we lose the life of our own.

Is global warming really coming
Or are the scientists wrong?
I ask myself these questions,
Do you?

Let's face it,
Everyone wants to do something before they die,
When I think about it,
I don't know what I want to do,
Maybe drive the Bugatti Veyron,
Maybe give blood
To someone who's losing their own,
Until that day,
I have a lot to think about.

Lawrence Luffman (12)
Bristol Cathedral School, Bristol

The End Of The World

It was starting to get cold
As the rain poured down
Smashing on the pavement
Like long, thin needles.

The thunder that seemed a million miles away
Boomed in the background
While the moon overhead
Hid behind the dark, stormy clouds.

The tree's branches
Were like long, spindly fingers
As they reached across the narrow, windy street
As though protecting it.

The street lights flickered
Into moments of darkness
So that the moon's dull glow
Replaced the light.

And as I sat there
I felt as though the world had ended
And the chill in the air
Filled my heart with despair.

Andreas Aristotelous (12)
Bristol Cathedral School, Bristol

The Match

Sweat trickling down my face,
Nerves tickling my spine,
I take a step forward, not knowing what will happen next,
Singing and chanting is heard,
My heart starts to pound, as I pull up my socks,
I can see that the other players are nervous too,
Their eyes are watering,
Bodies shaking,
But they can't quit now,
It's too late.

I hear my name called,
It's time,
I take a deep breath,
My legs shaking as I slowly stumble forward,
A small ray of light blinds me,
The ray gets bigger as I walk forward,
Suddenly, the chanting of the crowd becomes louder,
I try to speak,
No words are heard.

The walking starts to get faster,
The light is bigger and brighter,
I am shaking more than ever,
We erupt onto the pitch,
To reach the deafening roars of the crowd.

Georgia Wathan (12)
Bristol Cathedral School, Bristol

My Cat's View

I wake up to a dark room
I crawl out of my basket
I walk slowly up the dark stairs
I see a door
Can I get out?
Am I locked in?
I am!
They have trapped me down here
No food
No escape
I desperately jump and rattle the big, round, shiny thing
For help
Ah, my servant is coming and opening the door for me
I ask politely for my breakfast
She gives it to me
But then my servant comes down the stairs again
With a sharp, pointy thing!
I run for my life!
They grab me and then jab me!
Then they leave
I am tired
What a morning
Time to sleep.

George McCarthy (12)
Bristol Cathedral School, Bristol

Snowflake

Swirling, whirling, meandering down
Cold wisps of wind blowing me onward
Whistling through the skeletal treetops
The world to me encased in an icy shell
Black fingers of smoke coiling from houses
Pointing accusingly at the dark sky

Flutter past people in thick winter coats
Frantically running this way and that
Their movements and bustling pushes me onwards
Towards my final resting place

I find a lone house surrounded by snow
I can sense my journeying over
I limpet myself to a misty cold window
My journey is over, my journey is done

Coldly, clingy the frosty sun rises
Enveloping me in a golden glow
I feel the warmth running through me
Warming my icy crystals
I can feel myself turn to liquid
I run down the icy sill
I drip down onto the frosty grass
My beauty becomes one with the world.

Huw Grant (12)
Bristol Cathedral School, Bristol

Through The Eyes Of A Soldier

I never would have thought that these eyes would see the end
The thundering bombs still playing in my head, like a stuck record
But we still fought on
We had no choice.
The dead bodies increasing,
Every hour, every day,
Hear the distant cries.
My sister, my family,
Are they still alive?
I pray for the first time,
For my family, for my life,
But I must fight.
A tear runs down my hot, dry face
Now the bombs fall
And I can no more feel my body.
For the last I saw of this war,
Are my faithful soldiers,
Reaching out their hands to me.
I am now here,
Alive and well
And my family,
We have fought.

Isabella Salisbury (13)
Bristol Cathedral School, Bristol

Otters

As I slide off the steep, slippery bank,
Twirling, swirling, after the fish,
Rudder thwacking, jaws clacking,
Gaining steadily,
The fish is struggling,
As my elegant body slides closer,
Hunger closes in on me,
I claw at it,
It's in my grasp,
As I slide back to the riverbank,
The glorious fish in my mouth,
My sleek, shiny, slippery, gleaming, athletic body,
I dive into the water again,
The exhilaration of a chase kicks in,
I torpedo after it,
My sleek, elegant, athletic body,
The water gushing past me,
My fleecy, furry, agile body draws ever nearer,
My teeth clamp around it,
It's over.

Ross Geddes (12)
Bristol Cathedral School, Bristol

Sharks

I'm gliding, flying slowly onwards.

In the darkness that be my home.
Alone, cold and hungry!
I hear nothing except the rhythm of my emotionless heart.

I look greedily, carefully for my food.
I think where it could be.
I see something, I stop!
Then I slowly circle round and round, watching,
Staring, trying to identify and study this new prey.
Swimming, thinking faster and faster,
Hearing nothing but my racing heart.

I prepare, getting closer, keeping steady
 But always gaining faster and faster.
My eyes closed, jaws ready, trying to keep with the beat.

I go silent for a second that seems to last forever.
Snap! Snick, teeth tear!

I am full and now I go home.

Matthew Titcomb (12)
Bristol Cathedral School, Bristol

The Football Team

Everyone steps off the bus
Talking excitedly about the match,
Which they are all looking forward to
Except for me.

There is the opposition, over there,
A bunch of tough-looking thugs,
They can't be a football team,
They belong in prison!

'Now, listen up,' says our coach,
'Jimmy, go in attack, Joe, on the left,
Steven in goal, Mike in defence,
Let's score straight away.'

'And you,' he says, turning to me,
'If you get the ball by accident,
Pass it quickly, don't run with it,
We'll have you on the bench.'

The score is 2-2, with five to go,
When I get sent on in midfield,
Suddenly, the ball comes to me,
'Shoot!' everyone shouts.

I swing my boot as the ball comes,
I am only six yards out, I could score!
But I scuff it awfully and it goes wide,
That's why I'm the bench warmer.

Henry Lodge (13)
Bristol Cathedral School, Bristol

WWI

Bang! Bang! Bang!
Bomb! Bomb! Bomb!
Never stopping, never ending
Screaming, oh, the screaming
Mud, mud, please, no more mud.

Death looms in every inch, in every corner
Blood, blood, blood, endless blood
Stinging blindness, can't escape, can't hide
Hot and bubbly, coating the lungs and hardening
Breathing heavy, quick, quicker
Put on your suit and your mask.

Bang! Bang! Bang!
Gunfire
Where? Who?
Pain, pain, sharp pain
Silence
And peace once again.

Oliver Sullivan (14)
Bristol Cathedral School, Bristol

Blind Person

Darkness, coldness, only sound and touch
Why am I here?
Why can't I see?
Blind for eternity
Never seeing, never watching, never looking at people
People laughing at you
People hurting you
Having to touch
Having to use all my other senses
Having a friend, having a dog
Days with my dog
Then rain always raining and cold
The pitter-patter of rain on the windows.

Peter Dixon (13)
Bristol Cathedral School, Bristol

Whale

Twisting, turning, gliding, sailing,
Diving, plunging, swirling, twirling.

The sound of the water gushes through my ears,
As I emerge through the darkened sea.

The water captures me in its cool grip,
Tightens me and I push along the seabed.

The coolness of the water shivers down my spine
And I stop for a second.

I look back,
I can't turn back, I've got to go on.

The coral reef appears ahead of me now,
I've done it, I've made it.

Travelling for weeks and months,
My fins tired, drooping like spaghetti.

I'm home,
I'm back.

Saydee Rumbelow (12)
Bristol Cathedral School, Bristol

The Never-Ending War

The shells never stop coming
The cold, dense fear
The grip on my gun
The wait for help to come.

The dark arrives late today
Thank God I'm still alive
Life is a victory, I say.

Now the darkness sets in
The senses are dulled
No sight, no sound
God knows how we shall win.

But now the war is at an end
A great victory some say
But none think of the soldiers
Whose lives to their country, they lent.

James Clarke (12)
Bristol Cathedral School, Bristol

In The Eyes Of Sadness

No self-esteem, only self-doubting
No smiling, no laughing
Just sinking and drowning
Trying to fly up, but only falling down
Trying to scream out, but can't make a sound.

Hannah Javid (12)
Bristol Cathedral School, Bristol

Homeless Soul

It's a cold, rainy morning
Everyone is going to work
Cars zoom past me
A woman walks past me, like I am not there
Do I not exist anymore?

It's not my fault I'm here
My father kept hitting me
He wouldn't stop
My mum was screaming in the background
She was the only person keeping me alive
I had to run, he wouldn't stop.

Now I want to die
But I never manage to make myself do it
So I have to live with waking up every day
No food, no water and no money
I am dead.

Corin Ward (12)
Bristol Cathedral School, Bristol

The Day I Fell In Love

Hard to breathe, feels like floating,
So full of love, my heart's exploding.
My palms are dry, mouth is shaking,
My heart is yours for the taking.

I'm feeling scared, not myself,
Dancing around like some kind of elf.
Time; how it feels for this poor slob,
To know how it feels to fall in love.

Cameron Craig (12)
Chipping Campden School, Chipping Campden

Why Does It Matter?

When you stand face to face,
Why worry about race,
Be you black,
Be you white,
You all have a place.
When you're tall, you're too tall,
When you're short, you're too short,
If you're thin, you're too thin,
If you're fat, you're too fat,
Who's going to win?
There's a place in the world,
For the old and the young,
But the division between,
May never be won.
Stand out from the crowd,
You'll be one on your own,
But join up with friends
And you're never alone.
Wars will be fought,
Over religion and race,
We should learn to accept,
Each other in good grace,
Then the world would be a peaceful place.
We need the world to be a greener place
And wipe out all wars of religion and race.
The young, the old,
The black, the white,
We must all live in peace,
To put the world right

And then we'd be in a paradise!

Lauren Wright (13)
Chipping Campden School, Chipping Campden

What Is This World?

What is this world?
Twisted faces of the homeless littering our streets
And with all of the hustle and bustle we tend not to notice,
They cry out, but we walk on,
Is this the world we live in?

Skeleton features of the depressed, past caring,
We walk on, as it would be 'rude' to say something,
They silently scream for help, but what do we do?
Nothing, nothing, nothing,
Is this the world we live in?

A child cowers in a corner as they taunt her,
We try not to listen; we don't want to get hurt,
They spit out fireballs of stinging words,
Fat, ugly, ginger,
Is this the world we live in?

Animals shriek as another tree falls to the ground,
We just watch, scared of being challenged,
They run as they try to find a home,
They try, try, try,
Is this the world we live in?

People weep at the loss of a dear one,
We stand back, feeling sorry,
The coffin is lowered as the rain pours,
Drip, drip, drip,
Is this the world we live in?

What is our world?
A mirage of when we were happy,
We try to reach for it, but it is just a reflection,
We do nothing, scared of what will happen,
This is the world we live in.

Catriona Bone (12)
Chipping Campden School, Chipping Campden

Dorothy

I ran my pale, delicate hands
Along his cold, metallic face.
I longed to fill his body with warmth
So he could hold me close.

'Lend me your heart,' he said
'So I can love you with all of it.
I'll speak in kind words,
As you once spoke to me.

I'll lift you into my mind,
So you can understand
My soul, mind, body and heart,
As I long to understand yours.

We can lay in the poppy field
Of our dreams
And sleep until our minds
Merge into one.'

I took those gleaming red shoes off
For one last time,
I took my heart
And laid it on his harsh tin chest.

Feeling a coldness deep within,
As his body flooded with warmth,
He took me in his arms
And touched my black hair.

'Love can last a lifetime,
If it is forever mutual.'
His handsome voice did not
Penetrate my thoughts.

'But I cannot love without a heart.'

Samantha Boarer (17)
Knowles Hill School, Newton Abbot

We Like Dancing All Over The Place

Rolling Stones
They're good, aren't they?
Mick Jagger played, 'It's All Over Now.'
I'll tell you what their names are:
There's Charlie, Keith, Bill, Ronnie
And Mick Jagger, of course

It's a very old record
It crackles a bit
It's a very old recording
Very old pop
I like 'Up On My Cloud' and all that

I turn it over, on the other side of the record
Records are big
You put on the needle
Turn it on
It'll click at the end
You put it in the sleeve
The music's all gone.

Robert Lockwood (18)
Langside Special School, Poole

My Generation

Aeroplanes are flying
The environment is dying
War is growing
In Africa it's not snowing
The seas are warming
It's even warm in the morning
Terrorism is on the rise
People are growing in size
Animals are being killed
More and more we have to build.

Russell Peters (14)
Mangotsfield Secondary School, Bristol

Those Days

Those days when 'meanie' was the only insult,
Those days when we played 'pretend' predicting our future,
Those days when we went to the park,
Those days where grown-ups were tight,
Those days when the closest thing to a roller coaster was a slide,
Those days when Barbie was the best,
Those days when kissing was icky and boys were smelly,
Those days when Mum was the only one who said she loved you . . .

Those were the days, now they're gone,
Those were the days, what went wrong?
Time was wasting away, everything changed,
The pendulum swung too fast,
But now I realise nothing will last.

Ty Netherwood (13)
Mangotsfield Secondary School, Bristol

One Red Rose To Last Forever

Every time I look around,
I see you gazing at me,
Your lips move, but you make no sound,
That's just the way I want it to be,
Is this your salvation?
Is this all you can give?
You made my dreams come alive,
Without you, how can I survive?
Hand in hand,
Eye to eye,
We lay back to look into the sky,
I sometimes wonder why you love me,
Is it because everyone else hates me?
Every time when I come home,
You've left me a rose,
Today's will be the last;
One red rose to last forever.

Jasmine Pearce (14)
Mangotsfield Secondary School, Bristol

The Great War

The war to end all wars, they said,
So many injured, so many dead,
Blindly into battle were led,
Thousands of soldiers left wrong in the head.

Going to war, using a gun,
The prospect of this is only for some,
Getting bombed, *bang!* 'Run!'
Knowing your work will never be done.

Every soldier blazing with hate,
Why do they suffer such a horrible fate,
It leaves them in a traumatised state,
So really war isn't that great.

Kristina Chamberlain (13)
Mangotsfield Secondary School, Bristol

The Future . . .

My future is frightening,
What's the world to bring?
In debt as fast as lightning
And robbed in just one ring!

Lies, scams and betrayal,
Not just by your friends,
It's like an endless trail,
It's never going to end.

Computers will rule,
People will die,
Popularity falls
And people wonder why.

Everyone lies and cheats,
Humans are second best,
I wonder when this deadline meets
And this happens to the rest!

Louis Huxley (13)
Mangotsfield Secondary School, Bristol

My Generation

Did you see that boy today?
Standing on his own, wishing the world away
Hoping that somehow some miracle could save him from the pain.

They're laughing at him
Why would they commit such a sin?
They don't understand why he's alone.

He's waiting for a sign
For something somehow divine
To take him another way.

But there is no such thing

Like a bullet through emotions

He realises

There *is* nothing else

Nothing else to believe.

Jack Trickey (13)
Mangotsfield Secondary School, Bristol

My Generation

My generation is full of music,
Bands all make you wanna choose it.
The prices are such a scam,
I just lost my money, damn!
The high-pitched sound of a guitar,
Could end up smashing a jar.
The thumping sound of a bass,
Could wipe out a whole race.
Breaking a jaw on a piece of gum,
Is not as painful as a very loud drum.
Rock 'n' roll ain't gonna die!
Haters can all fry!

Charlie Stargatt (13)
Mangotsfield Secondary School, Bristol

I Remember . . .

I remember my first day at school,
Waking up at 5.00am thinking I was cool.
I wondered about all the things I would do,
Then I woke my mum with a monstrous *boo!*

I remember walking excitedly all the way there,
We could take in one of our toys, so I took in my bear.
The bell rang; it was time to go inside,
I was so excited for the amazing, wondrous ride!

I remember my mum going home,
I thought I was left all on my own.
I tried to join in with all the girls and boys,
Then we played with all our little toys.

I remember when break time came,
Lots of children asking me what's my name?
When break had finished I had a new best friend,
Wishing that this day would never end.

I remember the bell ringing, time to go home,
I didn't want to go, so I started to moan.
I told my mum about my wonderful time,
Then she said tomorrow I go back and learn rhyme!

Emma English (14)
Mangotsfield Secondary School, Bristol

War Poetry

I wandered around the dead,
The battle was won,
The lives were lost,
Would I be the same again?

My memories are shimmering in front of me,
I will not be right again,
I search for someone, fearing the worst,
My childhood friend lost on this field,

The dozen that have survived,
Wounded, injured, scarred for ever,
I passed someone I recognised,
Dead, gone, as I looked into the eyes that could not see,

At last, I found him, he was here,
I had never felt more alone,
With trembling hands I closed his eyes,
Then I placed my gun on his chest.

I could not leave him,
I felt a warm hand on my shoulder,
'It's time to go,' he said,
I left him, looking into his face for the last time.

Dan Hinsley (13)
Mangotsfield Secondary School, Bristol

Smoke

I'm trying to find out what you are, who you are,
Why you are as you are and not what I want you to be.

It all started out quite well,
With the summer sun keeping you sweet

And the compliments coming like sweet summer rain every day,
Like the trickle of temptation in the middle of May.

I quite believed your words, as they fell from your tongue and into
                                                                        my ears,
As you toasted to us that night, raising your glass, giving thanks,
                                                                         giving cheers.

Making me blush, making me smile,
Never knowing it was going to change into bitterness.

Deceiving is an art, they say,
Lying is a masterpiece,
You must be the artist of my world,
God knows you are crafted, as though by angels.

I'm trying to find out what you are, who you are,
Why you are as you are and not what I want you to be.

I guess I'd describe you as smoke, there one minute, gone the next,
A rare beauty to behold, but too much of you is deadly.

You choke my lungs and make them tight,
You keep my eyes watering, all through the night.

You linger in the room; your touch stays on my clothes and hair,
When I most want to forget you, that's when you're most there.

Smoke comes from something good,
A birthday candle, the warmth of fire,
Smoke is the after-effect,

I guess what we had was good,
Summer sun, love and laughter,
I guess you're what's left over
And I guess I'm what's left here.

Amy Joyce (14)
Mangotsfield Secondary School, Bristol

Broken

He hides in his mind,
Doesn't open up,
Never letting out,
Thought driving inward,
Madness driven out.

Keeps himself locked up,
All happy times forgotten,
Sinew, bone, it's all intact,
But mind is unsound, rotten.

No one hears the scream inside,
No one ever hears a sound,
No one knows anything's wrong,
But inside he is crashing down.

His mind is cracked,
His voice is meek,
He is so pathetic,
His soul is weak,
But now his blood has stained the floor,
It's splattered on the bathroom walls,
His body is still, he's as cold as lead,
He gave up that day
He is now dead.

Patrick Dennehy (13)
Mangotsfield Secondary School, Bristol

Christmas Day

I remember on a snowy Christmas Day,
Dragging a sack of presents through the hallway,
Gently placing my sack on the ground,
I opened the top and guess what I found . . . ?
I remember the old, shattered, white snowman,
Laying helpless on the lawn,
His hat, scarf and buttons awaiting another winter's dawn.
I remember the snowflakes trickling on my face,
The smell of hot turkey and vegetables on my plate,
I glanced at my watch, the day was going fast,
I thought in my head, *I wish it could last.*
The hours clocked by and my stomach filled,
The snow continued to fall and the windows chilled,
Unfortunately, the time had come to go to bed,
But at least I had the memories secure in my head.

Joe Weston (13)
Mangotsfield Secondary School, Bristol

War Poem

We were sitting inside a lorry,
Trying not to worry,
I didn't know what to do,
But I wanted to pull through.
The large truck came to a standstill,
I hoped I didn't have to write my will,
When an Iraqi found us there,
He gave me a horrible stare,
Escorted us, holding his gun,
So no one dared to run,
In a rotting room we sat,
Dreading the gory combat,
Every day they gave us food,
That never changed our mood,
So I started writing
And hope everyone stops fighting.

Neal Goodman (13)
Mangotsfield Secondary School, Bristol

I Remember

I remember . . .
That Ashes winning team of 2005,
That *bang* as Kevin Pietersen hit a massive six,
That *snap* as Freddie Flintoff smashed the middle stump in half,
That *roar* as England fans rejoiced every run and every wicket
And that *cheer* as Michael Vaughn lifted the Ashes trophy
On that beautiful English day.

I remember . . .
The English fans celebrating the Australians' misery,
The England players parading around a joyous Trafalgar Square,
The publicity that cricket received all over the world
And the funding cricket teams all over England got
From the Cricket Association.

I remember . . .
The humiliation of that whitewash in the 2006 Ashes,
The misery coming from the Australians' joy,
The high expectations, having to wait another year
And the disappointment of the inadequate performance.

Oscar Ryan-Reed (14)
Mangotsfield Secondary School, Bristol

Jabbermockry

(Inspired by 'Jabberwocky' by Lewis Carroll)

Was Saturday and the match ball,
Did slip and slide in the rain,
All slippery were the tunnel walls
And the players all so vain.

Beware the football boots, my son,
The toes that kick, the studs that cut,
Beware the seven-foot beast that runs,
The monstrous hard nut.

Abbey Smart (14)
Mangotsfield Secondary School, Bristol

Daddy's Gone To War

Mummy says Daddy's gone
She says he's gone away
I hope he's gone somewhere nice
Like when we went on holiday

I asked Mummy where he went
And how long was he going to be
She said he went far, far away
And as for coming back, we'll see

Daddy wrote me a letter
He sent me a photo too
In the photo he stood by a tank
And the letter said, 'See you soon'

Daddy has been gone a year
He's coming home today
Mummy's driving up to meet him
Come back from far, far away

Mummy's car came home without him
She said he didn't show
I guess we'll just have to wait
For Daddy to come home

Today we got a letter
It came through the post
It made me cry a lot
But Mummy cried the most

The letter said some bad news
It said Daddy wasn't coming back
I asked Mummy who killed him
She said one word . . .

Iraq.

Claire Fudge (14)
Mangotsfield Secondary School, Bristol

My Pen

As I wrote my essay,
I read it through,
Shakespeare's interests were,
Sitting on the loo.

Then it said,
'I hate you,
Love me or release me,
What you choose.'

I then chose,
The pen went mad,
I started to panic,
This was bad.

My pen said,
'I'm going to shout!'
I replied,
'That I doubt.'

My pen grabbed,
A big football,
Threw it at the teacher,
'Alex! Forty-five after school!'

I could not win,
I let it go,
As he went,
His eyes began to glow.

Alex Bryant (14)
Mangotsfield Secondary School, Bristol

Talkin' 'Bout My Generation

A lonely child wanders
Through the sunset sky
The world spins round, the sun goes down
The child starts to cry.

The tears roll so gently
Down the child's abandoned face
The cruellest monsters on this Earth
Are no doubt the human race.

The child grows so hungry
Soon, he will starve
As he stumbles down the busy street
People look and laugh.

Inside him there's a message
In which he needs to share
You're playing with a child's life
This ain't no truth or dare.

Two lonely children wander
Through the sunset sky
The Earth spins round, the sun goes down
The lonely child and I.

Tom Berkeley (12)
Newent Community School, Newent

Talking About My Generation

We are youngsters
Most of us like football
Most of us like having a laugh
We don't mean to hurt people

I believe
You should be polite to everyone
You should help people
Manners don't cost anything

I think
Old people can be afraid of youngsters
We might smash a window
Or we might be rude to them

I don't believe in vandalism
I don't believe in terrorism
I just believe in *education*.

Michael Barry (15)
Notton House School, Chippenham

A Generation Forgotten

Forgotten is the way of the world now
With your fast beating music and your fast paced cars
It feels like yesterday that I was in the trenches with gun in hand
Because I believed I could save this godforsaken land
All you do is go to pubs and clubs
Hyping yourselves up on psychedelic drugs
I hope you're happy in your generation of fun
Because now I'm in the generation of the forgotten.

Joel Johnson (14)
Notton House School, Chippenham

Scarred For Life

The horrifying scene in front of my eyes,
I watch as my companion gets shot and dies,
Bombs going off, releasing lime-green gas,
I fumble round my neck to find my mask.

Its cold metal surface sends a chill down my spine,
As I pull my feet together and step into line,
Then I turn left and see, in front of my eyes,
A blood-coated body, covered with flies.

The sirens are wailing, shots being fired,
I trudge on, though my legs are tired,
Bombs booming, shouts and screams,
The world shatters around me, or so it seems.

I swig my water as my mouth is dry,
So bland, so tasteless, yet it keeps me alive,
Longing for food but there's no time to stop,
So I carry on marching through the foul-smelling slop.

Exhausted from the journey and scarred by the sights,
I begin to tremble, as I fill with fright,
A bomb has gone off not far away,
In my heart I am shocked, but I need to be brave.

As I take a breath in, through my nose,
The smell of fresh blood grows and grows
And as I take a glance up to look at the moon,
I realise this nightmare will be over soon.

Holly Woodrow (12)
Oldfield School, Bath

Tamed Angel

Light shone, so bright, enough to feel wrong,
Take down the moon and create the sun,
Get rid of the pain, the suffering and the wrong
And in its place, let harmony flourish.

She waits and sees it all,
She sits and runs her pale fingers through her black hair,
Her dark eyes open, filled with sadness
And her beauty radiates onto the hate-filled world.

A swirling, heart-stopping abyss,
A bottomless tunnel,
An aching, bleak horror,
Filled with pain, not meant for Earth.

Dearest Angel, tell me why,
Why aren't you helping?
Tell me why you're hiding,
Please, dearest Angel, tell me why.

Soft and gentle, her black satin-soft wings open,
Caring for everything and feeling for them,
She cares for everything and feels for you,
She takes the strongest of hearts in a breathtaking touch,
She shows us dreams of a better world.

The sun will shine,
The stars will twinkle
And the world will be free,
The wind will chase laughter across the green fields,
The scent of happiness will caress the Earth.

Meg Ryan (14)
Paignton Community & Sports College, Paignton

The Latest Fashion Accessory

The latest fashion accessory,
Some school are known for it,
Seeing their primary pupils parading around,
Feeling 'in the know' of the fair fashion industry,
Being 'popular' and feeling 'smug' that their
Friends haven't got one and they have.

They change social societies,
To those who have also acquired the new
Fashion accessory in this clothes-conscious world.
Others are left equally envious,
As their friends,
One by one, acquire the latest accessory,
Wondering who they can bribe to achieve one for themselves.

Teachers look on in green jealousy
And dismay at 'last season's' accessory:
A reject.
A 'what's not this season',
To the ever-changing criteria of 'what's hot'.

Like I said,
Some schools are known for it -
Seeing their primary pupils parade
Around with the latest, longer-lasting styles
Sashaying off them,
However, this new fashion accessory will last longer.

Regardless of 'what's hot or what's not',
With the latest fashion accessory
These primary pupils
Will have first class experience in
Health class.

Katie Cleanthous (18)
Paignton Community & Sports College, Paignton

The Crying Of The Soldiers

The crying of the soldiers
The rattling of the gun
This is the war
Not some pitiful fun

The cowardly ideas
Of running well away
What would people think of me?
I really cannot say

My father would reject me
My mother would ignore me
My lass would divorce me
I need some re-enforcement

I'm sure I'm going to die
Some day, somehow
The world will collapse on me
The world will forget me

I don't believe in God
But maybe it's time to,
My heart, my soul, my body
It's all going to you

The crying of the soldiers
The rattling of the gun
This is the war
Not some pitiful fun.

Sam Pembery (12)
St Bede's Catholic College, Bristol

My Generation!

Talking 'bout my generation
Hi-tech things and immigration
Forget the afros
It's all ASBOs

I don't care for the baker's name
All I need is a PC game
My phone's a pebble, not a brick
I don't care if you call me thick

Schools are no more the same
Except that they are so lame
No more holidays down in Kent
The USA is where I went

I'm fed up with cows and sheep
All I need is a poodle to keep
Yep, that's my generation
We're sweeping the generation.

James Bishop (12)
St Joseph's Catholic College, Swindon

Chocolate!

The sweet, fine taste
The lush, daring mouthful of eating it
It would be so bad to put it to such waste
To chomp on it, bit by bit
Looking at the dark-coloured substance
Taking one glance
Boom!
I'm after it
It makes my eyes drop
But I'm out of reach
Although, then again
I could just pop down to the sweet shop!

Michael Fawcett
St Joseph's Catholic College, Swindon

Talkin' 'Bout My Generation

Aston Martin's down my street,
New music with a heavy beat,
Supermarket's at my door,
Some people eat wild boar!
No more cane in school anymore,
Everyone fighting in worldwide wars.

Population increasing fast,
New movies with a quality cast!
Old people worried about climate change,
Whilst we're making cars strange,
Old people couldn't play,
In the facilities we have today!

Ralph Lauren and famous brands,
Old people talk about family clans,
Cocaine, heroine, fags and druggies,
Babies being pushed around in buggies,
Everyone lovin' the football federation,
This, my friend, is my generation!

Cameron Gordon (12)
St Joseph's Catholic College, Swindon

Waiting

In the trenches, from morning till night
I lay there, ready to fight
Reading my letters with some memories
With my rifles sat next to me
Shivering in the cold, dark ground
Lying there underground.

Waiting for the enemy
I can feel the fear all around me
Some men smoke, some just stare
The smell of death is in the air.

Alana Turner (15)
St Joseph's Catholic College, Swindon

Talkin' 'Bout My Generation

My generation is big and new,
All of me - none of you!
I'll have a good time,
There'll be no more crime,
This, is my generation!

My generation is mighty and proud,
Music blaring, really loud!
My clothes are bright, with chains hangin' down,
Causing you old fogies to give us a frown,
This, is my generation!

My generation is a jubilation,
Clearing up your devastation!
For you, things are very strange,
All these things, like climate change,
This, is my generation!

You were once young,
With slang from your tongue!
If you just give us a chance,
This world, we'd enhance!
My generation - just give us a rest,
My generation - we're the best!
My generation - my population,
My generation - *my generation!*

Gavin Cowie (12)
St Joseph's Catholic College, Swindon

Flicking Pages And Paper Cuts

My tears are falling down my face
I stare out the window in disgrace
You left me alone
In a dark, cold lie
And everything I said to you
I think as I cry

My love for you is nothing now you have gone
I might as well give up, it's all gone wrong
The lie you told me
The pain I was in
Was all for you, I never win

A dusty book fell off my desk
Photo album is what it said
Flicking pages
Paper cuts too
Until I found the page of me and you

What a pain it was to see your face
I threw the book into my case
It will never take back the things you said
Just the way you treated me, I'll never forget.

Abigail Finneran (15)
St Joseph's Catholic College, Swindon

Mum And Dad

Mum

Mum, your warm face to me
Is like the morning sun
You are my ray of light when skies seem grey

When I need food, shelter or a helping hand
You are always there, by my side you stand

Forever and always you'll be my mum,
I'll remember your face in the morning sun

When I get angry, shout and fight,
You're always there to set me right

Your loving hug when I am ill
Much better than a doctor's pill

These thoughts are all too often unsaid
Forever locked up inside my head

But now is the time to get the key
And say just what you mean to me

So, thank you from your loving son
Mum, you're my morning sun

Dad

Dad, you are my life support through tough times
You fight for me, care for me, teach me

If I need something done
I know that I can come to you

You work hard to succeed well
I know that I want to be you, can't you tell?

Mum says we're too alike
Crazy together for all of life

My dad, the best of them all
We have disagreements, we have our fights
But overall, you're always right

At the end of the day, you're my dad
And I'm glad to call you

My dad!

Gary Rains
St Joseph's Catholic College, Swindon

To Dream Or Not To Dream

As I lie sleeping
In my bed
Dreaming of clouds
Above my head
Floating through dreams
Or so it seems

My blanket so warm
My mattress so soft
Nothing in my way can harm
As we all float aloft
My dreams are wondrous
I wish my dreams were ponderous

I hope it's soon when
I will start dreaming again.

Tim Reuby (14)
St Joseph's Catholic College, Swindon

Bugs

Bugs, bugs, go away,
Bugs, bugs, always in the way.

Some are big, some are small,
When they crawl under my door,
Some are hairy, some are not,
Hiding in the flowerpot.

As I'm driving down the motorway,
Bugs are flying in my way,
Splatting on my windscreen,
Later I will have to clean.

When I hit them they will go away,
If I *splat* them, if I *squish* them,
If I hit them with one shoe
Or maybe I will need two.

What a mess they can make,
Flat as a pancake, they will make.

Yellow pus,
Oh, what a fuss!

Alex Wood
St Joseph's Catholic College, Swindon

Our Generation

Stop dissing our generation
It's our youth, our jubilation
We were all kids once as you know
Just cos our similarities don't show

So yes, we've got video games
With stupid, flashy, silly names
Our clothes are too big and scruffy
With boots that are orange and fluffy

Just cos we don't get the cane
And our lessons aren't the same
We all are full of languages for chattin'
But all you oldies learnt was Latin

Us kids have one thing to say
We all will be adults one day
So stop trying to rudely shun
Our lives, our ways of having fun

So stop dissing our generation
It's our youth, our jubilation!

Gabrielle Liddiard (12)
St Joseph's Catholic College, Swindon

The Beast

There he was, the deadly beast,
Eating an enormous feast,
There she was, my lovely mum,
Devoured right down to her bum.

He cracked her bones and squeezed her legs,
As if they were some boiled eggs,
Her brain he mashed with milk and malt
And added just a pinch of salt.

Her skin he mixed with bread and jam,
Her eyes resembled jelly,
That's not the last of it,
You should see her belly!

I saw this with my very eyes,
I never said my last goodbyes,
It makes me sick to think of it,
That horrible, rotten beast!

Rebecca Morgan (15)
St Joseph's Catholic College, Swindon

Untitled

Friends are there forever,
Not just whatever,
They come around and make you smile
And they even go that extra mile.

You're never there alone,
They're always down the phone,
You could never clone them,
They are your gems.

You always have fun,
Especially in the sun,
They always make you laugh
And help you choose a path.

They know the way to take you
And the way to make you,
You talk to each other all the time
So I thought I'd make a rhyme!

Rebecca Hooper
St Joseph's Catholic College, Swindon

Someone I Know

There is someone I know
Who is feeling rather low
They've been given some news
Which put them in a mood

When they told people the news
They burst out crying
They thought they might lose
One of the most important people in their life

They can't sleep at night
Too many thoughts
They can't find the light
Confused and shaken to the core

Scared about leaving family behind
Wondering how they will cope
Without them being around
They think he feels duty bound.

Zoe Checchia (15)
St Joseph's Catholic College, Swindon

Untitled

You are here, in my heart
In reality, we are so far apart
I have been crying to myself
I believe it's messing with my health
Confused and annoyed
Upset and destroyed
This isn't me
This is what you made me be
My head's in a mess
People think it's just stress
I don't believe it's true
My parents don't know I know about you
This is really hard to take
Soon I'm going to break
I can't see you here
Please tell me you're near
What if when I find you is never
Does that mean you're lost forever?

Holly Fuller (14)
St Joseph's Catholic College, Swindon

I Hope You Know

Do you see me?
I do not know
Am I just a friend?
I do not know

But guess what I do know?
My feelings for you will never change,
Through rain and wind and snow
My feelings will never be rearranged,
Though, although I feel this way
I'm also ever so hurt,
Because as I scuff my shoes in dismay
Over mud and stones and dirt,
I know you'll never belong to me
It makes me ache inside
I know we'll never be

So, whenever you see me,
I hope you know
It's thanks to you
I cried

It's thanks to you,
The life inside me died,
The things you do,
The way you talk
The way you make me blush
The way you walk
The way you make my blood rush
My blood pound,
My heart throb

Do you see me?
I do not know
Am I just a friend?
I do not know.

Sara Conway
St Joseph's Catholic College, Swindon

Mobiles

Mobiles?
Well, what can I say?
They're here,
There,
There,
No, there,
Everywhere!

'No mobiles at school'
That's not what I heard!
People always have them,
In their back pockets,
In secret pockets,
In their blazers,
In their hands.

In class I listen,
Then I look around,
Unamazed I see,
He's got his phone out,
So has she
And her
And he.

But what are people doing with them
Out all the time?
Socialising, that's what!
They text
And text
And text some more!
Well, I suppose that's my generation for you,
Ain't it?

Peter Keighley (14)
South Molton Community College, South Molton

Street Lights

Walking down the streets,
Staring at the ground,
There's nothing, except for rubbish
And lights shining down.

Music, rap, rock and pop,
Never-ending till the break of dawn,
Broken bottles line the pavements,
People dressed for a night of fun.

Shops closed for the night ahead,
Security men guarding entrances,
Alarms on house doors,
Keeping elderly people safe inside.

The night's soon over,
When people return home.

Shopping centres open,
Fashion starts to sell,
Short skirts and skinny jeans,
With dolly shoes covering the shelves.

New technology stacked up high,
Laptops, MP3s and games,
Mobile phones made more complicated,
Thinner, slicker and smoother.

Fast food many times a week,
Lunch, dinner, all the time,
Supermarkets to get everything you need,
No bakers, butchers or greengrocers.

Ice caps start to melt,
Polar bears and penguins at risk,
All because of the people today,
Not caring about what they do.

Laura Short (14)
South Molton Community College, South Molton

I Am Just A Kid

Are we killing the world,
The animals, the plants, the people?
Will it be my fault
If they all die?

Why do we do bad things?
Steal things, break things and hurt other people?
Does it give us adrenaline?
Should I try it?

Am I a chav?
Are you a chav?
Are we all chavs?
What is a chav?

Does the Internet rule our lives?
Can we live without it?
What would happen
If it wasn't there?

Why are we at war all the time?
Is fighting right or wrong?

Why do people take drugs?
Does it make them feel great?
Take the pain away?
Should I take drugs?

Is my generation wrong?

Laura Dennis (13)
South Molton Community College, South Molton

My Generation

Brought up well-mannered,
Polite and honest,
But at the age of only five,
My parents separated,
Moved school often,
Met lots of new friends,
Taught the ways of the world,
Murder, rape, you know the rest,
We hear stories,
On the television and radio,
See new designs,
Groups and technology,
Large family
And lots of support,
I've managed through the years,
With laughter and tears,
Things can be hard,
But I've got my dad
And all my mates
And I live life to the full,
Now and forever.

Kate Carter (13)
South Molton Community College, South Molton

My Generation

My generation
Has a reputation
For being bad
And making people mad
No matter what you do
Everyone puts the blame on you
It's so unfair
They don't even care!

Bryony Zeitzen (13)
South Molton Community College, South Molton

Start Gate

The white cotton-like stuff on the peaks of mountains,
Strapping two planks to your feet and flying down the hillside,
Going up the ski lift, awaiting your place in the competition.

The nerves bubbling till they fill your whole body,
Your feet go numb,
Your arms feel heavy,
Your knees start to shake.

You get to the start gate,
The final beep goes,
You forget to push off,
That's where the race is won or lost,
The start gate.

Cameron Cree (13)
South Molton Community College, South Molton

Being A Teenager

Every day passes
Lessons to be learned
Opportunities passed
Now I'm stuck in class

Today I learnt love
Or why it's never true
'I love you'
I really, really do

Is it true from me to you?
Do I really love you too?
You stole my heart
Like fine art

You're perfect, clever, smart

We're perfect together
Me and you.

Jack Smith (13)
South Molton Community College, South Molton

Mountain Biking

A man leans down
To pick up his gun

He then loads it
And lifts it up to the sky

On top of the mountain
At dusk

Things are getting ready
To happen out of sight

The tracks are built
Nerves are building up

At the starting line
One bike is black
One wheel is as green as grass

The line drops
Brakes are off
And they're off
Down the mountain.

Louis Hardy (12)
South Molton Community College, South Molton

My Generation

My generation started a long time ago,
I can't quite remember that far back though.

When my parents were young, they didn't have cool stuff,
Like computers, cars, gadgets and phones,
So I guess they got bored and started to moan.

So their parents got cross
And started to boss.

I wonder what it was like back then?
Probably hung around with people aged ten!

Beth Taylor (13)
The Cotswold School, Cheltenham

Our Generation

People say our generation is made out of:
ASBOs, recycled plastic, rugby, alcohol and drugs,
But is it really that?
Or does it consist of:
Love for our country,
Having fun!
Changing the world,
Having Young Enterprise to make
Our community a better place!
Well, to be honest,
No, not at all!
Our generation is:
Mobile phones,
Size zero,
Jack Wills,
Vans,
Gangs,
Fashion,
Laziness,
Idleness
And of course, rock 'n' roll!
That is our generation!
OAPs complain about our generation,
But why should they?
It's not theirs, it's ours!
That's why it's called . . .
Our generation!

Camille Smith (12)
The Cotswold School, Cheltenham

Will The New Generation See Me?

Can't you see me?
Am I not like any other child?
Working since age five
And have never smiled

Don't you care?
I could die!
Can't you hear
My silent cry?

Would you rather tell yourself
It will be OK
And all this
Will go away?

New technology
A new generation
More wealth
But more separation

There you stand
And here I lie
Living in luxury
While I scrape by

A new hairstyle
The latest fashions
Matted hair
Living on rations

Music, phones, games
And education
Illness, poverty, sanitation
And segregation

Can you hear me?
Is this the new generation?
Do they see me?
Or am I just in their imagination?

I've always been here
I always will be
Living in poverty
Please . . . someone help me!

Hannah Davis (14)
The Cotswold School, Cheltenham

My Generation Poem!

My generation care a lot
Even if they get a spot
The girls love fashion
The boys have passion
For playing lots of sports
While the girls do all sorts
So next time you say to us
You look lovely, no need to fuss
We shall reply nice and sweet
'Stay out of this, go read 'Heat''
I am going to meet my crush
So get out of my way, I'm in a rush
In the end, it doesn't work out
On the phone we begin to shout
Broken-hearted is not strange
Then it turns into rage
Here's my point you should know
Leave my generation alone!

Natasha Surch (13)
The Cotswold School, Cheltenham

Today's Generation

My generation,
Is full of good and bad,
Global warming, natural disasters,
It can make people sad.

There are ASBOs and yobs
And goths, they're all crazy,
But are youths of today,
Just plain rude and lazy?

They can be harsh to their families,
Sisters and brothers,
Or they can be kind
And try to help others.

They're involved in student councils,
Take part in recycling,
But the things they get up to,
For parents, is frightening.

So why do they do it?
Why grow up so fast?
It's the best time of your life
And it doesn't last.

Your parents tell you stories,
But what are we to say?
Don't copy me son, but,
I shot someone today.

It's extremely hard,
Living in this damnation,
But the youth's mischief,
Is today's generation.

Lee Salf (14)
The Cotswold School, Cheltenham

Sun Through A Ruined Sky

The end, or is it?
No caring in life
Death do we visit

No self-control
Drugs and thugs and
Tattered soul

Lose the goodness within
Men of hate and
Soldiers of sin

Why should we care?
With fights at home
With Dad never there

But there are those who try
Bringing the sun back
To our ruined sky

The nameless in the city
Dying full of
Admiration and pity

Sun through the ruined sky
My generation
Saviours in a lifeless lie
My generation.

Ben Brown (13)
The Cotswold School, Cheltenham

Our Generation

People say our generation's lame,
Instead they like people with lots of fame.

But without our generation,
How would we have found out about fashion or sport?
Because they used to wear really short shorts.

How would we have run our towns?
And how to earn lots of money and act like the class clown.

How would we have found out how to deal with trouble?
But now we have built jails which hopefully
Won't end up in a load of rubble.

They found our future leaders and rock 'n' roll,
Because they invented shops and malls.

We now have lots of killers and robbers on the loose,
Who run around like a crazy moose.

Without our generation would we be alive?
Or would he just be bees in a hive?

OAPs think our generation is bad,
But I think they are going loopy and mad!

Claire Fisher (13)
The Cotswold School, Cheltenham

Technology

Kids these days - all they want is new technology,
Trust me, listen and you will see . . .

Jimmy wanted an Xbox 360,
But his dad still hadn't paid the debt off the plasma TV.

Jimmy wanted a Nintendo Wii,
Whereas his mother wanted to go to Austria to ski.

Jimmy wanted an Apple Mac,
So his dad paid the money to get a smile back.

Jimmy wanted an iPod video,
But was actually surprised when his dad said,
'No!'

Louis Millar (14)
The Cotswold School, Cheltenham

Is Love The Word?

Married couples on the street,
Proposing men at women's feet.
Crying mums at primary school,
First day children keeping cool.
We all need love, me and you,
Without love, what shall we do?
There are kids far and wide,
Who don't get love, they have to hide.
For what? You are asking me,
Cannot be found, it's hard to see.
But if you look into their eyes,
A heart of love slowly dies.
Hungry, thirsty, on their own,
This poor child has no home.
We need to help our generation,
Please stop pain and segregation.

Laura Martin (14)
The Cotswold School, Cheltenham

So, What Do They All Know?

So, what do they all know?
So what if we're Goth, Chav or Emo,
It is our fashion,
It is our passion,
So, what do they all know?

Popularity, single or taken,
Disagree? You must be mistaken,
'Cause this life is mine,
To live and to shine,
So, what do they all know?

Today's youth is well-measured,
Curfews, ASBOs are not to be pleasured,
But maybe we're all just misread,
Or maybe you're just being misled,
So, what do they all know?

Lauren Castleton-White (13)
The Cotswold School, Cheltenham

Teenage Generation

Life is a game
World full of thugs
Petty thieves gaining fame.

Parents not in control
Sons and daughters with ASBOs
Drugs taking their toll.

Soldiers made to fight
Violence and abuse at school
Destruction at first light.

Blood in the park
The territory, war continues
The fight goes on in the dark.

This is my generation
But not my life
Life in damnation.

Matt Gibson (13)
The Cotswold School, Cheltenham

A Typical Online Game

My pals and I were sitting in a cave,
One said, 'Think he'll ever appear?'
I laughed out loud, 'Balrog takes a while,
I'm going to kill some lizards with my spear.'

I stabbed my foes, crushed my enemies,
None of these stood in my way,
I drank a potion and felt my strength return,
But then my friend had something to say.

'Quick! Come quick! We need you now,
We're fighting a Balrog in here!'
I shouted, 'OK!' and ran to the scene
And immediately attacked with my spear.

It barely flinched, then turned and attacked,
I was sent flying away,
I drank a potion and felt my strength return,
But then my friend had something to say.

'I'm out of power! Elixir, *now!*'
My friend weakly held his staff,
I was too slow; Balrog killed him in one,
My other friend evilly laughed.

With a cry for the dead, I raised my spear
And struck Balrog as hard as I may,
Balrog flinched, yet struck me again,
But then my friend had something to say.

'Keep it up, man, I've got your back!'
He launched some arrows into the air,
With the last of my strength, I struck the beast
And we defeated Balrog right there.

I felt myself become stronger,
I no longer had to wait.
'Yes! Level up!' I cried aloud,
I now knew that this game was great!

Odin Anstiss Liljefors (14)
Torquay Boys' Grammar School, Torquay

My Generation

We are the masters
Of this great nation
We don't need no plasters
This is my generation

Playing on my Xbox
Three Si-i-ix-ty
Oh yeah, come on, this rocks
Playing on Guitar Hero III

We are the masters
Of this great nation
We don't need no plasters
This is my generation

Going out with my mates
We're gonna play rugby
Someone cries, getting hit in the face
What a geeky pansy!

We are the masters
Of this great nation
We don't need no plasters
This is my generation

Going to the corner shop
To get some sweets and cans
On the way the geek tells our parents
Aw maaaaaaaan!

We are the masters
Of this great nation
We don't need no plasters
This is my generation

Lots of chavs on probation
This is my generation!

Charlie Hill (12)
Torquay Boys' Grammar School, Torquay

Talkin' 'Bout My Generation

iPod Nanos and PlayStation 3s
(Talkin' 'bout my generation)
It's stereos and HD screens
(Talkin' 'bout my generation)
If you think you'll find anyone
(Talkin' 'bout my generation)
Outside, having good old-fashioned fun
(Talkin' 'bout my generation)
You're wrong

This is my generation,
This is my generation, baby

While global warming melts the poles
(Talkin' 'bout my generation)
There's mass extinction from pandas to whales
(Talkin' 'bout my generation)
All that matters to people is wealth
(Talkin' 'bout my generation)
No consideration for care or health
(Talkin' 'bout my generation)

This is my generation
This is my generation, baby

Everyone's aware of status
(Talkin' 'bout my generation)
Whether it's a flashy house or a brand new Lotus
(Talkin' 'bout my generation)
There's an unbelievable amount of poverty
(Talkin' 'bout my generation)
Round the globe from Vietnam to Malawi
(Talkin' 'bout my generation)

This is my generation
This is my generation, baby.

We can feed the world, we can stop those wars
(Talkin' 'bout my generation)

House the homeless and open new doors
(Talkin' 'bout my generation)
Fix the ozone with scientific armoury
(Talkin' 'bout my generation)
We'll strive for peace and harmony
(Talkin' 'bout my generation)

This is my generation
This is my generation, baby
My generation.

Matt Carr (14)
Torquay Boys' Grammar School, Torquay

Detention

First day of school and I'm back,
I've got my books in my rucksack,
Ten minutes in and I've been caught,
I've been told off, cos my tie's too short.

5x6 our first sum
And I've been caught out chewing gum
Stole Mr Jones' house key,
What the heck, I got a DT.

I dropped my choco bar on the floor,
I did it in French cos it's a bore,
I swung a punch at Lee,
'Oh no!' Not another DT!

It's geography now, lesson three,
I can't believe it, I need a pee,
I said, 'Stuff global warming prevention',
For that I got another detention.

Science was last,
My chloride went blast,
Mr Roberts wasn't happy with me,
For that, I got one more DT.

Tom Charlton (13)
Torquay Boys' Grammar School, Torquay

My Generation

M ost people think Chavs are 'sound'
Y oung gangs hang around the town

G ame consoles are taking control
E very town has police on patrol
N ever have I seen so much pollution
E veryone trying to find a solution
R acing cars are now in fashion
A nd no longer do Chavs have passion
T hugs are often carrying a gun
I diot teens find fighting fun
O verdosing on drugs is not rare
N ot many people think the world is fair.

Jay Cooper (12)
Torquay Boys' Grammar School, Torquay

The Real World

Our life is not fair,
Our life is not good,
It's the people around us,
Who don't treat us like they should.

It's their thunderous hearts
And their destructive flame,
That makes us feel heartless,
When they are to blame.

So everyone out there,
Who feels this grief,
Call out to the darkness,
For a cry of relief.

We'll fight them together,
We'll fight all night long,
They can harm us no longer,
For unified, we're strong.

Xennor May (14)
Torquay Boys' Grammar School, Torquay

House the homeless and open new doors
(Talkin' 'bout my generation)
Fix the ozone with scientific armoury
(Talkin' 'bout my generation)
We'll strive for peace and harmony
(Talkin' 'bout my generation)

This is my generation
This is my generation, baby
My generation.

Matt Carr (14)
Torquay Boys' Grammar School, Torquay

Detention

First day of school and I'm back,
I've got my books in my rucksack,
Ten minutes in and I've been caught,
I've been told off, cos my tie's too short.

5x6 our first sum
And I've been caught out chewing gum
Stole Mr Jones' house key,
What the heck, I got a DT.

I dropped my choco bar on the floor,
I did it in French cos it's a bore,
I swung a punch at Lee,
'Oh no!' Not another DT!

It's geography now, lesson three,
I can't believe it, I need a pee,
I said, 'Stuff global warming prevention',
For that I got another detention.

Science was last,
My chloride went blast,
Mr Roberts wasn't happy with me,
For that, I got one more DT.

Tom Charlton (13)
Torquay Boys' Grammar School, Torquay

My Generation

M ost people think Chavs are 'sound'
Y oung gangs hang around the town

G ame consoles are taking control
E very town has police on patrol
N ever have I seen so much pollution
E veryone trying to find a solution
R acing cars are now in fashion
A nd no longer do Chavs have passion
T hugs are often carrying a gun
I diot teens find fighting fun
O verdosing on drugs is not rare
N ot many people think the world is fair.

Jay Cooper (12)
Torquay Boys' Grammar School, Torquay

The Real World

Our life is not fair,
Our life is not good,
It's the people around us,
Who don't treat us like they should.

It's their thunderous hearts
And their destructive flame,
That makes us feel heartless,
When they are to blame.

So everyone out there,
Who feels this grief,
Call out to the darkness,
For a cry of relief.

We'll fight them together,
We'll fight all night long,
They can harm us no longer,
For unified, we're strong.

Xennor May (14)
Torquay Boys' Grammar School, Torquay

Terrorism

Every day one is born,
So there is no time to mourn,
Creating trouble is their deal,
The world is their meal.

Every day one is born,
To cure the land,
That's their job.

However, to others they seem like God,
Freeing their country of their troubles,
Terrorists or freedom fighters?
It's your choice to decide.

Stop it now,
Before they realise their next ploy,
Ruining the lives of people.

Karan Purewal (12)
Torquay Boys' Grammar School, Torquay

Politics

Why I pay any attention to politics,
I don't know at all,
It's not a normal thing to do,
It may even be uncool.

'Why should you care?'
People say,
'Why should you listen
To the confusing mumbles
Of the politician?'

Of course,
I'm not on anyone's side
And why should I be?
They are all politicians.

Jack Fletcher (13)
Torquay Boys' Grammar School, Torquay

I'm Not Your Generation

My generation: doesn't stand in line
My generation: doesn't have the time
My generation: doesn't listen to you
Most of my generation: doesn't get the connection to The Who
My generation: doesn't want grown-ups trying to be cool
Your generation: thinks we are fools.

My generation: are trying to make up for you burning fossil fuels
My generation: more are wearing diamonds and jewels
My generation: the difference is growing
My generation: the money is slowing
My generation: you don't understand
My generation: eventually, we'll be in demand.

Lewis Rowden (14)
Torquay Boys' Grammar School, Torquay

Will We Ever Get Along?

Do we all just muck around
And leave our rubbish on the ground?

Yes, that's what you people think,
You think we smell, you think we stink.

We listen to iPods, play games every day,
That's what you think, but actually . . .

There's more to our lives than just music and games,
In fact, compared to you, we're nearly the same.

We have the same feelings, emotions as well,
So why do we make each other's lives Hell?

We'll be with you for ever and ever,
So can't we just learn to live together?

Michael Curran (14)
Torquay Boys' Grammar School, Torquay

Terrorism

Every day one is born,
So there is no time to mourn,
Creating trouble is their deal,
The world is their meal.

Every day one is born,
To cure the land,
That's their job.

However, to others they seem like God,
Freeing their country of their troubles,
Terrorists or freedom fighters?
It's your choice to decide.

Stop it now,
Before they realise their next ploy,
Ruining the lives of people.

Karan Purewal (12)
Torquay Boys' Grammar School, Torquay

Politics

Why I pay any attention to politics,
I don't know at all,
It's not a normal thing to do,
It may even be uncool.

'Why should you care?'
People say,
'Why should you listen
To the confusing mumbles
Of the politician?'

Of course,
I'm not on anyone's side
And why should I be?
They are all politicians.

Jack Fletcher (13)
Torquay Boys' Grammar School, Torquay

I'm Not Your Generation

My generation: doesn't stand in line
My generation: doesn't have the time
My generation: doesn't listen to you
Most of my generation: doesn't get the connection to The Who
My generation: doesn't want grown-ups trying to be cool
Your generation: thinks we are fools.

My generation: are trying to make up for you burning fossil fuels
My generation: more are wearing diamonds and jewels
My generation: the difference is growing
My generation: the money is slowing
My generation: you don't understand
My generation: eventually, we'll be in demand.

Lewis Rowden (14)
Torquay Boys' Grammar School, Torquay

Will We Ever Get Along?

Do we all just muck around
And leave our rubbish on the ground?

Yes, that's what you people think,
You think we smell, you think we stink.

We listen to iPods, play games every day,
That's what you think, but actually . . .

There's more to our lives than just music and games,
In fact, compared to you, we're nearly the same.

We have the same feelings, emotions as well,
So why do we make each other's lives Hell?

We'll be with you for ever and ever,
So can't we just learn to live together?

Michael Curran (14)
Torquay Boys' Grammar School, Torquay

Community Performs A Mutiny

Go out on the street and all you see,
Is hobos chewing old meat from a tin.
Walk further down to the old corner shop,
You shall find robbers being taken away by the local cop.

Turn left and walk around the car park,
Beware the Chavs racing cars in the dark.
Carry on, now with a quicker pace,
So as not to get caught in the nuisance made.
Round the bend and across the street,
Carry on going, hoping not to meet.
Turn back home and you find teenage girls getting paid;
Wonder what they've been up to - hmm, getting laid.

Get back home, pick up the phone,
Talk to your friend.
'Our community,
Should perform a mutiny.'

Johnny Foster (14)
Torquay Boys' Grammar School, Torquay

Life - My Generation Is Unique

M y generation is unique.
Y our generation is unique.

G enerally, I like it this way.
E mos, nerds, Chavs, all different.
N ot everyone however, is like this.
E verytime someone interferes, someone disturbs others.
R eal life is like that; it's not always right.
A person is a person though; they have a reason.
T o kill someone for getting in the way of your life is wrong.
I n reality, you are the one who suffers, even though
                                           they are gone.

O ne question: *is this fair?*
N ot mine to answer . . .

Jack Oades (13)
Torquay Boys' Grammar School, Torquay

What The Future Holds

The kids laze around their homes,
Playing on computers and mobile phones,
Their mums constantly trying,
To get them outside, but fail and end up crying.

With new technology and machines,
New cinema companies like 'Pearl and Dean'
All kids do is watch TV screens,
Not like the old days where they made up the scenes.

Outside you find the gangs of today,
Who have nothing to do but cause dismay.
Hanging around starting fires,
Damaging things and deflating car tyres.

Living on fast food and fizzy pop,
Ignoring their parents when they're told to stop.
From this I conclude that the generation of today,
Will be unfit, obese and end up in a very poor way.

Ben Hustwayte (13)
Torquay Boys' Grammar School, Torquay

What Sport?

The oval ball twists and turns
Sprinting around while calories burn
Around a player sprinting for the line
What a good tackle, now the ball's mine.
A spinning pass, a high cross kick,
Powering through, but who will catch it?
The crowd are cheering, urging me on
They try to tackle me, but I'm already gone
The whole team is cheering my name
Rugby, that's the name of the game.

Calum Luke (12)
Torquay Boys' Grammar School, Torquay

Us 'N' Them

Our generation has so much to say,
It's always evolving and still is today.

Year after year we've been slated and praised,
Our hopes have been dropped and then have been raised.

We've achieved so much and come so far
Yet we take things for granted, do we deserve a star?

Money and food and clothes on our back,
We take them for granted, that's not opinion, that's fact!

We're put under pressure with stuff like SATs
And get yellow cards for acting like prats!

We're all made to feel like we need to be genius,
But get ripped to shreds about the size of our p****!

But there's no doubt we have contributed
And no one could be better suited.

So, whatever you do, don't make a fuss,
Just think about . . . just think about us!

Rowan Naidoo (14)
Torquay Boys' Grammar School, Torquay

Youths And Yobos

Us teens, are always bored,
We ain't interested unless it has a cable or cord.

Kids are hooked on video games,
It's not our fault, but we are the ones to take the blame.

I spend my weekends walking around,
We get kicked out of somewhere and try to rebound.

But it's too hard to do the same old thing,
When there are chavs everywhere shining their bling.

We have nowhere to go, nothing to do
And we'll be doing the same until we find something new.

Matt Woods (14)
Torquay Boys' Grammar School, Torquay

War

War has been going on for thousands of years,
But still today, it brings the most tears.

With bombs, missiles, guns and mines,
Being used on the innocent so many times.

The world is being drawn apart,
Like slowly destroying a good piece of art.

Many are dying by no fault of their own,
Their villages destroyed, no place to call home.

People waiting in fear for the next bomb to drop,
They just keep on coming, there's never a stop.

This pain and torture just can't go on,
If it continues we all will be gone.

Without help the war will not end
And everyone's lives will never, ever mend.

Jasper James (13)
Torquay Boys' Grammar School, Torquay

The Environment

Only when the last bush is burnt
Only when the last flower's trampled
Then will we realise you can't eat money

Only when the last ocean's drained
Only when the last spring dies
Then will we realise you can't drink silver

Only when the last birds are killed
Only when the last tree is cut
Then will we realise you can't live off gold

Only when the last fish dies
Only when the Earth is dying
Then will we realise
Diamonds aren't forever!

Yussef Robinson (12)
Torquay Boys' Grammar School, Torquay

The Youth Of The Country

The youth of the country,
Hasn't improved very much,
With the drugs and the killings
And all of the stereotypes.

They are getting into trouble,
Even more than before,
They are getting arrested or stabbed,
By the fuzz or the gangs.

They're staying out late,
Getting drunk and having fights,
Some of them get really rowdy,
When others just get down and dirty.

So the youth of the country,
Isn't the best in the world,
But I've only mentioned the bad bits,
For the youth of the country.

Chris Robson-Close (13)
Torquay Boys' Grammar School, Torquay

The Future Is Changing

The future is changing,
Disaster is in the air.
Fear of future shakes the air,
Red mist clouds our eyes.
The world is changing,
Suffering here and there.
Pain is everywhere.
Cool places get cooler,
Hot places get hotter.
As a society, we are all murderers,
Murderers of happiness.
The news is full of hatred,
The papers full of death,
The future is changing.

Harry Morse (12)
Torquay Boys' Grammar School, Torquay

Ebay

Ebay is really, really cool,
You can buy anything, even a mule,
If you can't buy a spare key,
Find one on Ebay and get one free!
Ebay.com is the place to go,
To find a Ferrari if your car is slow,
If you're bored, give Ebay a try
And the next day, you'll wonder what to buy!

Alistair Roberts (14)
Torquay Boys' Grammar School, Torquay

New Generation

I've written this poem,
'Cause I wanted to show 'em,
The people that always know the answers,
Who think they're so much better than the rest of the chancers.

These people are old-fashioned
And their meanness should be rationed,
'Cause they keep on moaning
And they should have better toning.

Together they are grown-ups
And they make us wash their cups,
Yet we let this madness continue,
But inside, we are annoyed too.

The penultimate fiasco,
Is that we are always the last to know,
Complaining is not our nature,
But it will be worse later.

The final affliction,
Is that while telling us our restrictions,
They have caused global warming
And now poisonous gases are swarming.

Steven Ford (13)
Torquay Boys' Grammar School, Torquay

Google

G rowth throughout the World Wide Web
O pened up a chance and so
O ver in America
G uys made up a marvel to
L ink up the Internet so
E veryone knows everything.

Mark Portnoi (14)
Torquay Boys' Grammar School, Torquay

Pollution

Destroying our planet
Over our nation
All throughout our generation
As our world crumbles
Whispers are mumbled
It's evolution
However . . . it's pollution

Trash cans and litter
Cover our streets
It's always there . . .
We always meet
So help us save Earth
Or else we'll be cursed
With a world full of junk
And a universe that's sunk

So, listen carefully
Earth will die
Now is that what you want?
And do not lie

So, help us today
Or we'll fade away.

Henry Lister (13)
Torquay Boys' Grammar School, Torquay

Talkin' 'Bout My Generation

Xbox this and PS3 that,
Google searches in point-two seconds flat.

DS here, PSP there,
Crowds of people arrive to stare.

Xbox 360s apparently jokes,
Just like eggs without the yolks.

PS3 are they the kings?
But worth more each than golden rings.

Gangs of chavs with all their bling,
Even though it's not worth a thing.

What are you, a chav or a goth?
A geek, an emo or just a boff?

Where shall we eat? Burger King or Maccy D's?
Pizza Hut, Subway or KFC?

Tom Owens (13)
Torquay Boys' Grammar School, Torquay

Survivors

Did they have TV?
What did they use to research?
Where were LEDs?

Where is caning now?
What about home deliv'ry?
Where were microwaves?

They are survivors,
The adult generation,
Without luxuries.

Iain Tinkler (14)
Torquay Boys' Grammar School, Torquay

My Generation

Technology ever growing
With laptops and PS3s
There's even virtual rowing
And massive widescreen TVs

This is our generation

Everything's always changing
Like new rules for ev'ry sport
Ping-pong changed to pong-ping
And football played with a bat I bought

This is our generation

Lots of new genres of music
Like Indie and electronic dance
Many new tunes for you to pick
Sounds around us change and advance

This is my generation!

Jake Wilkinson (13)
Torquay Boys' Grammar School, Torquay

Football

Football is the best,
United, Liverpool and
Then there's all the rest.

Goal! Living the dream,
Gerrard, Rooney and Owen
Getting paid too much.

The awesome World Cup
And Premiership title
The dream cups to win.

Josh Reilly (12)
Torquay Boys' Grammar School, Torquay

The Hitman

With the guns in my bag,
I watch your every move,
To find out your position,
I use the mark of your shoes.

With my eye in the scope,
The rooftops I wait,
Unless you stay protected,
I will end your fate.

To make you scared,
I will shoot at your feet,
It will be torture
And we will meet.

My prey can run,
But he can't hide,
I stalk in the shadows
And stand by his side.

The victim thinks he's safe,
I will take his life,
In his house I wait,
With a sharpened knife.

He walks in the door,
Upstairs I hide,
But later that night,
He will have died.

He lays awake,
I give him pain,
I kill him relentlessly,
The Hitman's my name!

Lloyd Barwood (13)
Torquay Boys' Grammar School, Torquay

The Future's Bleak

There are muggers and thieves in every back alleyway
It's not safe, not at night, not at day
There's a hobo in almost every bin
Their food, old meat from a tin
PlayStation, an immortal power
More popular than the Eiffel Tower.

My generation, the future's bleak
It won't get any better throughout the week
Another day, another night
Will our generation see the light?

For the elders, there's no respect
The children they can't reflect
The reason is very clear
Murderers and muggers live on every street
The only thing they know, is the sound of feet.

My generation, the future's bleak
It won't get better throughout the week
Another day, another night
Will our generation see the light?

My generation, in them there is some good
Make the world a better place, they know they could
The future's gonna be alright
It won't change overnight.

Luke Breyley (14)
Torquay Boys' Grammar School, Torquay

My Life

Fourteen now, it's a great year,
Not yet old enough for some beer

Some of my friends have an ASBO
But I prefer my teacher's KLASBO
(Klassroom Anti-Social Behaviour Order)

Hanging round with a posse
Boy, I wish my teacher was not so bossy

Do you do what your parents say?
Do you instead, go outside and play?

What will you do when you get old?
Do you not want to go bald?

What's it like in the future?
Will there be a new computer?

What will we do when the oil runs out?
How do you think we'll get out and about?

So, I have one more thing to say
Go out and enjoy the day.

Nathan Gilpin (14)
Torquay Boys' Grammar School, Torquay

A Mother's Complaint

My son's generation don't listen to me,
They're all too busy on iPods and Wiis.
Hanging out on the street, with chavs, emos and punks,
Listening to rock music, rap, hip-hop and funk.
He phones up his mate to talk about 'stuff' for a while,
Discussing who's got the latest mobile.
My son's generation don't care how Britain's run,
All they really care about is just having fun!

Joe Reed (14)
Torquay Boys' Grammar School, Torquay

Getter Older

In our generation, there's a new life
With all of the youth on the street
In all the towns where they are
It's hard not to see police on the beat

As technology starts to take control
And the PS3 and the new Wii
Are taking over most kids' minds
Where's the old English scones and tea?

The UK's population starts to build
And the schools start to fill
And kids are starting to become illiterate
They could start on the pill

As they get older and find a job
They seem to lose some hope
Their flats are trash covered in junk
They sit around and mope on dope

Our generation is not like it was
Where's Shakespeare and his "twas'?

James Tucker (12)
Torquay Boys' Grammar School, Torquay

My Sports

M aking the crowd cheer
Y ou shoot and score

S weat dripping down your face
P ing-pong is great and fun
O verhead smash, your opponent's nowhere
R ugby ball flying around
T ennis racket big and round
S port is the best!

Phil Reddaway (12)
Torquay Boys' Grammar School, Torquay

Talkin' 'Bout My Generation

Why, oh why, is there smog in the sky?
It's ruining our Earth and making us cry,
Why, oh why, are there planes up above?
I mean, why can't we see a beautiful dove?

Why, oh why, is the ozone going?
It's much too hot and the rivers aren't flowing,
Why, oh why, are the ice caps fleeing?
I don't quite believe what I am seeing.

Why, oh why, are the rainforests dying?
It makes me so sad, I feel like crying,
Why, oh why, are all these trees falling?
And all the time the government's stalling.

Talkin' 'bout my generation,
Causing a pollution infestation,
Talkin' 'bout my generation . . .

Rob Harris (13)
Torquay Boys' Grammar School, Torquay

No Hope

The crazy urban sprawl,
Screams of anger now,
Toxic gases rule,
Biased political polls,
Hooked on online war,
Imagination's torn,
Mindless generation,
Dark and grey nation,
Hooded thugs rule,
Kids taken for a fool,
Certain death,
Streets on crystal meth,
No hope,
No love,
But it's my generation.

Kieran Hill-Cousins (13)
Torquay Boys' Grammar School, Torquay

Not Our Time

Climate change and wars
Bans against 4x4s

Tony Blair leaving power
The collapse of the Twin Towers

Lots of gang crime
This isn't our time

With all the pollution
Where is the solution?

Drinkers on a binge
Society on a hinge

Police always on the beat
We all bask in the heat

Children now can't be smacked
This really is a fact

However much these are said
My generation is in my head.

Edward Lovell (13)
Torquay Boys' Grammar School, Torquay

Technology

Technology is getting better,
They say,
But is that really true?
Cos hey!
All this generation have phones
And these TVs
And all this technology is leading,
To increasing brain disease,
Their minds get baffled,
Their eyes go square
And to be honest,
No one really cares.

Henry Booth (11)
Torquay Boys' Grammar School, Torquay

Computers Will Control The World!

One day, computers will control our race,
Exploring the mysteries of deep, deep space,
They'll do the things we used to do,
Like football, PlayStations and eating too!

They'll venture into realms unknown,
But they'll never be able to whine or moan,
Because they're only computers, computers that's all,
Anyone could stop them, even a school!

But they're not all that tough,
They're not waterproof,
They don't heal,
They don't feel pain,
A drop of water could frazzle their brain!

Dan Ponsford (12)
Torquay Boys' Grammar School, Torquay

The Lazy Gamers!

All my generation,
They make up the nation,
Most have beer bellies,
For they sit in front of tellies.

Three-year-olds play 'Saint's Row',
So soon they'll get an ASBO,
They boast if they've got iPods,
But really, they are little slobs.

They sit around playing video games,
Not caring for their anxious mums,
Not sleeping, eating, even bleeping,
Just transfixed upon their bums!

What happened to books?
Peter Pan and Captain Hook?
About celebrities' road to fame,
But no . . . it's *stupid games!*

Alex Dyer (11)
Torquay Boys' Grammar School, Torquay

Homework

Homework ain't at all that great,
It's just a waste of time and space,
English, maths and geography,
I'm telling you, it ain't easy.

Every night, it's in your face,
I know that it is a disgrace,
Teachers pile it on and on,
I just cannot cope anymore.

Here comes half-term and a break,
From homework and work all day,
But what do they do? They give us more,
It's getting worse than even chores!

Daniel Paton (11)
Torquay Boys' Grammar School, Torquay

Running

The race begins
I'm off at last
Yes! I'm winning
My mate's not fast

I've had a good sprint
And won't go slow
I've done a good 20
Only 80 to go

I've left them behind
No joke, I'll win
No one can beat me
I'm winning this thing

I've crossed the line
It's over at last
Then the horror
I had a false start!

Graeme Tinkler (12)
Torquay Boys' Grammar School, Torquay

The Phone

Ring,
Ring,
Ring,
That's what the old ones did,
Now with a phone
You can have it as a kid.
Computer, camera, diary
It's all there,
But hang on a minute,
My friend is texting me from somewhere.
So, even though adults
Might afford the best,
You can still be ahead
Of the rest,
Because no matter
What fancy phone they've picked,
They can still so easily
Get it nicked!

Alex Bird (12)
Torquay Boys' Grammar School, Torquay

Computers

Computers, computers,
They hold all of your information,
In everyday use,
Evolved by years,
Into PlayStations.

Computers, computers,
Used to crack codes,
You can chat to your mates,
Go online
And can be set to different modes.

William Sambells (12)
Torquay Boys' Grammar School, Torquay

Rise Of The Potter Series

Harry and his friends,
Hermione and Ron Weasley,
J K Rowling wrote,
It could not have been easy!

From the classic book one,
The youngest of them all,
To the amazing book seven,
Which saw old Voldi' fall!

All of them are amazing,
Your emotions will be heard,
But if you speak to Granger,
She'll write down every word!

At the end of the series,
When JK could write no more,
I enjoyed them all,
Certainly not a bore!

Joseph Fath (12)
Torquay Boys' Grammar School, Torquay

Rock Music

Rock music has a thumping beat
It makes me tap my dancing feet,
Rock music makes me feel so alive
It makes me want to jump and jive.

I like to listen to rock bands
Hearing their sound whilst I clap my hands,
Electric guitar, vocals, not forgetting the drum
Singing, whistling and eagerly trying to hum.

Going to rock concerts is a special treat
A lot of noise, not to mention the heat,
Taking in the atmosphere of the crowd
Bright lights, electric music and extremely loud!

Harry Loader (12)
Torquay Boys' Grammar School, Torquay

Talkin' 'Bout My Generation

The TV screen is on,
I watch my favourite show,
I stare and stare and stare and stare
Till my vision starts to go.

My mum steals the remote,
As I am almost blind,
She creeps around the sofa
And takes it from behind.

She puts on Channel 4,
Cos Hollyoaks is on,
After six hours of watching,
Her brain power is gone.

My sister puts on MTV,
As her mother has gone numb,
She then gets up to dance,
Wiggling her bum.

She then starts singing badly,
My ears now start to hurt,
I run into the garden and
Fill my ears with dirt.

The telly-box is guarded,
By my sister's watchful eye,
My brother turns the TV off,
What a stupid guy!

My sister's eyes are flaming,
Her face also goes red,
My brother realises,
That he will soon be dead!

Ben Hetherington (11)
Torquay Boys' Grammar School, Torquay

My Future

Really want to go to Mars
Where I'll invent flying cars.
I'll whip Federer, of course
Then I'll buy a robotic horse . . .

This is my future!

I'll enter an intergalactic race
Then whizz through outer space.
I'll make a fab cancer cure
Which is 50% cow manure . . .

This is my future!

I'll discover life on Mars
Before I disappear among the stars . . . !

Tom Godwin (11)
Torquay Boys' Grammar School, Torquay

Two Youths

People in their houses,
Scared like little mouses,
Running from gangs,
On the wall they bang,
Threatening, killing,
As if it is thrilling,
Dead, dying,
No one is trying,
To stop this from happening,
What happens is flattening,
This is the truth,
The youth,
Looks scary,
Not everything is our fault,
Not all of us are taking money from a vault,
We're left with a curse
And it hurts.

Carl Johnson (12)
Torquay Boys' Grammar School, Torquay

Technology

Kids today have so much stuff,
From the computer router,
To a first person shooter.

There's a load of consoles,
From a PlayStation2,
To a Wii 'cause that's new.

Some of the games are good,
So they play 'em all the time
Like the game Metroid Prime.

People can make them do anything,
They then do stuff really cool,
That is unbelievable.

I play video games every day,
I think that they're really fun,
Especially the games that I've won.

Technology today,
It has helped more than we could,
So that's why I think it is good.

Tom Fullalove (12)
Torquay Boys' Grammar School, Torquay

Why?

The world is full of worry
Everyone is in a hurry
All the adults hurry

Must we be told what to do
But the kids have their own crew
When we have a life, let us do what we can do

When we come home from school
All we hear about is the war pool
A pool of blood, flowing into a flood

The girl on the corner is crying
She hopes she is dying
Her whole life has gone flying

I stepped out of the door and walked down the street
Then a man walked up to my feet
He pulled a gun, it looked fun

He left me for dead
Little more than bread for the birds

Why?

Ronan Yeo (11)
Torquay Boys' Grammar School, Torquay

My Generation

Riding round in flashy cars,
Shooting rockets up to Mars,
Flying round in outer space,
Driving in a F1 race.

My generation,
My generation,
This is my generation.

Listening to iPods,
Not using fishing rods,
Always using mobile phones,
All we do is moan.

My generation,
My generation,
This is my generation.

Walking round eating fast food,
It puts you in a mood,
Playing in the filthy street,
Kicking footballs with your feet.

I'm talkin' 'bout my generation!

Kieran Brookes (11)
Torquay Boys' Grammar School, Torquay

Before I Die

Before I die
I wish to complete
The challenges
That I'd like to meet!

Firstly, I would love
To train to be a
Great policewoman
Who could save the day!

Next, I would love
To tour the whole world!
I want to see
The world all unfurled!

After, I would love
To see the day of glory
When poverty is
Just a distant story!

Lastly, I would love
To know that war
Is long gone and
We will see it no more!

Before I die
I wish to complete
The challenges
That I'd like to meet!

Kate Rowbottom (12)
Torquay Grammar School for Girls, Torquay

Music

Classical, pop, hip-hop, soul
R 'n' B, country, rock and roll
These are a few of the music crew
That everybody listens to.

Classical is sometimes really slow
But other times, fast and fun
Pop is cool and sounds great in a big hall
Hip-hop is funky and allegretto.

Soul dates back to the 50s and 60s
Country is like that too
R 'n' B is my favourite of them all
It's modern and it sounds new.

Last we have rock and roll
There isn't a lot to say
It's loud, it's busy and suitable
And we still love it to this day!

Bethany Pearce (12)
Torquay Grammar School for Girls, Torquay

A Flowing Brook

My generation is like a brook
Flowing on and on,
Over mirror-like stones,
Through ups and downs,
Droughts and pollution,
The brook flows on and on.

Eventually, all of us
Will reach the sea,
Where everyone will greet us,
My generation is like
A beautiful brook
Striving to reach life's sea.

Marina Scholtz (12)
Torquay Grammar School for Girls, Torquay

My Dream World And Me

M y dog eats my homework
Y ou all think I'm not popular

L iving in the dream world
I have created for my protection
F inish off my maths work
E at some food and go to bed

A ll my worries float away
N o one can hurt me today
D o some revision for my test

E very day I go to school
V ery tired and oh, so bored
E verybody walks by me
R ight and wrongs driven into me
Y ou all look at me
T hinking that I'm not special
H orrible RE stuff to remember
I n my dream world
N o one can hurt me
G otta go now, to my dream world.

Alexandra Searle (11)
Torquay Grammar School for Girls, Torquay

A Dream Come True

Looking up into the sky,
I wonder if I'll ever fly,
Looking at the gleaming moon,
I wonder if I'll get there soon.

Looking up into the night,
I've waited so long to be on this flight,
Now it's launching, 10 . . . 9 . . . 8
I'm so excited, I just can't wait!

Daisy Shirley (11)
Torquay Grammar School for Girls, Torquay

My Generation

The people of our era,
Are slowly led astray;
They are violent and vicious
And don't care in any way.

They are often far too loud
And frighten young and old,
They don't respect their elders
And don't do what they're told.

They are lonely and sad,
Depressed and often shy,
It is hatred and anger,
That consumes them up inside.

Their time and talents are wasted,
As they patrol around the streets,
Their deaf ears do not listen,
To the sirens of defeat!

Many people think this,
But actually they are wrong,
The youth of my generation,
Are the ones who will stand strong.

We do have self-respect,
We try to do what's right,
We just need love and time
And then you'll see our light!

Rebekah Cockram (12)
Torquay Grammar School for Girls, Torquay

So . . . This Is The 21st Century . . .

Sharing fashions, gossiping
Sleepovers and laughs
Make-overs and pampering
Soaking in the bath!

This is the 21st century . . .

PlayStations, Xboxes
Computers and Wiis
Playing football in the park all day
And having chips for tea!

This is the 21st century . . .

Working in their jobs all day
Not stopping for a break
Drinking lots of cups of coffee
How long will this task take?

This is the 21st century . . .

Girls, boys and maybe adults
This is their lives
Soon they will be married
Some kids, a husband or a wife!

So *this* is the 21st century!

Megan Dorrans (12)
Torquay Grammar School for Girls, Torquay

Life?

Why is there life?
                To save our souls?
                To break our hearts?
                To help the needy?

Why is there life?
                To ruin the world?
                To obey God's word?
                To be a good person?

Why is there life?
                To make technology?
                To learn about the past?
                To predict the future?

Why is there life?
                To make some money?
                To learn about us?
                To walk all day?

Why is there life?
                To be a lover?
                To have good children?
                To be a family?

Why is there life?
                To save our souls?
                To break our hearts?
                To help the needy?

Or is it all just for fun?

Chelsea Mitchell (12)
Torquay Grammar School for Girls, Torquay

If I Ruled The World . . .

If I ruled the world . . .
    Image wouldn't mean anything,
    Beautiful wouldn't mean best,
    Fat wouldn't mean sad.

If I ruled the world . . .
    Rubbish wouldn't mean waste,
    Recycling wouldn't mean a chore,
    The ice caps wouldn't mean history.

If I ruled the world . . .
    Cancer wouldn't mean lost,
    Old age wouldn't mean death,
    Drugs wouldn't mean helpless.

If I ruled the world . . .
    Clean water wouldn't mean a journey,
    Drought wouldn't mean hunger,
    Third World wouldn't mean poverty.

If I ruled the world . . .
    Children would mean free,
    Family would mean together,
    Wealth would mean sharing.

The whole world united, equal and happy . . .

Katie Needham (13)
Torquay Grammar School for Girls, Torquay

The Teenage Years

Out on the street,
The people you meet,
Are all rated,
Either good or bad,
Everyone's slated.
No need to hang your head in shame,
Everyone plays the same old game,
Boys breaking hearts,
Girls falling apart.
Drink and drugs,
Sex and thugs,
Parties late at night,
Always end up in a fight.
Chavs on one side, emos on the other,
What else can you do,
But run to your mother.
Then there's school,
Five times a week,
But I'm far too cool,
Too cool to be a geek.
The second I leave the school door,
The weekends are what I live for,
Messing around with mates,
Going on dates,
Spending money,
Then Mum calls - 'Where are you honey?'
'I'll be home soon . . .'
But I know for a fact I won't be.
But it all adds up in the end,
Even if things seem they'll never mend.

Daisy McArdle & Georgina Watt (13)
Torquay Grammar School for Girls, Torquay

My Life

Every day I'm cold,
With no possessions to hold.
Every day I'm hungry,
With only porridge to feed me.

My family and I,
Try not to cry.
For we live in a place,
Of utter disgrace.

Every day I walk,
With no shoes on my feet.
To the small river,
Filled with things that slither.

The river is dirty
And not very clean.
The colour is brown,
Which makes me frown.

One set of clothes,
Maybe a pair of shoes,
Is all I own,
But most of it I've outgrown.

My life is tough
And very rough.
But at least I'm alive,
Still trying to survive.

Bethany Day (12)
Torquay Grammar School for Girls, Torquay

If I Ruled The World

If I ruled the world
Equality would be cool
No more poverty
That would be the rule.

If I ruled the world
Far fewer planes would fly
Holidays taken nearer home
And birds would rule the sky.

If I ruled the world
Peer pressure would be out
Designer labels vetoed
No more bullying without a doubt.

If I ruled the world
Wastage would be less
No carrier bags, more recycling
We'd cut down on mess.

If I ruled the world
Love, peace and hope I'd promote
No more anger or fury
So, please give me your vote.

Emma Singleton (12)
Torquay Grammar School for Girls, Torquay

The 21st Century

This is the 21st century,
Everything new and bright.
With music on your mobile,
Laptops as thin as paper.

This is the 21st century,
Everything's hi-tech.
From Bluetooth through to MSN
And short'nin' words 'n' textin'.

This is the 21st century,
Species dying out.
Some because of hunting,
Most because of no habitat.

This is the 21st century,
Everything new and improved.
But have things really improved
Or is this just a rouse?

This is the 21st century,
Tell me what you think.
Has the world changed for good,
Or has everyone just gone crazy!

Ami Leanna Hardy (12)
Torquay Grammar School for Girls, Torquay

Regrets Of An Old Man

I sit here as a tired and lonely man,
When once to travel the world was my plan,
I really want to get up and go,
But like a tortoise, I am too slow.

When I was younger, when I had a smile on my face,
I would be the fastest in the running race,
I kept on going, I wouldn't stop,
On and on until I reached the top.

They were all so proud, Mum and Dad, I mean,
To see that I was so keen,
I showed my skills in other ways,
By cooking meals that would amaze.

All I can do now is sit and watch the TV,
I even have to ask the nurses to put on a DVD,
I am tired of sitting here doing nothing,
I wish I could actually get up and do something.

But soon my time will be gone,
I wish I could get up and carry on,
But still . . . I sit here a tired and lonely man,
When once to travel the world, was my plan.

Hannah Schofield (12)
Torquay Grammar School for Girls, Torquay

If I Ruled The World

If I ruled the world,
Things wouldn't be just as they are,
They'd be very different
And here's how they'd start.

Music would be top of my list,
Then maybe sport and friends,
If I could change a few little things,
The world would start to mend.

Having fun would come up next
And sweets and pop and parties,
There would be loads of things to do,
If there wasn't any boundaries.

We wouldn't need to go to school,
Maybe . . . once or twice a week
And we wouldn't really need to worry,
That our minds were getting weak.

But really, I wouldn't need to change,
Any of the above,
'Cause I know now that things as they are,
I'm really starting to love!

Evie Reed (12)
Torquay Grammar School for Girls, Torquay

What Does Life Mean In My Generation?

What is the meaning of life . . . ?

Love - is that what life truly means?
Truth - is that what it means, to always be true to yourself?
Yourself - is that who you should think about
        Or should you think about others?
Others - is that who you should care about?
        Would you sacrifice yourself for another's life?
Life - is that the most precious thing in the world?
The world - doesn't everyone want world peace?
Peace - isn't that the same as happiness?
Happiness - that's what I think we all need.

Darcey Roberts (11)
Torquay Grammar School for Girls, Torquay

Running

Running up and down,
A very long street,
Never, ever stopping,
To the constant beat.

My heart is racing faster,
With every single step,
I try to control it,
But I keep losing my breath!

Harriet Rowden (12)
Torquay Grammar School for Girls, Torquay

Why?

Why do I have to see the world
Through the eyes of a modern-day teenager?

Why do my eyes
See only war and death?

Why do they so rarely see love and hope
That guides our way along the windy way that is life?

Why don't I weep
At the sight of it?

Why does death come as a fatal blow
But hope never really shows?

Sarah Stoyle (12)
Torquay Grammar School for Girls, Torquay

And All For The Boy

G irls get stuck in all of the fashion,
E yeliner becomes our greatest passion,
N ice, pretty hair is all we care,
E yelashes should not be short and bare,
R uthless and daring is our new stride
A nd it's all for the boy on our right side,
T ittering and giggling is all we do,
I nitially we watch our friend get through,
O bviously in a mood and permitting no joy,
N othing gets in the way of getting the boy!

Emily Attwood Bloomfield (11)
Torquay Grammar School for Girls, Torquay

Poverty

Longer and longer,
Day and night,
They wait.
I'm glad it's not me.

Innocent lives are ruined,
Bringing a tear to their eye.
Black and white, all over the world,
Poverty changing lives.

Aching and aching for food,
Watching their family die.
Trying to rid these pangs of pain,
That are eating them alive.

No clean water in their wells,
They have no sheep or cattle.
Clinging on to every hope,
But fighting a losing battle.

Have no one to comfort them,
All alone they wait in vain.
There is no one to hear their cry,
Or the screaming of their pain.

These people are in poverty,
Whilst we sit in our ivory tower.
The past we can no longer change,
But the future is our power.

Longer and longer,
Day and night,
They wait.
I'm glad it's not me.

Jo Thorpe (11)
Torquay Grammar School for Girls, Torquay

Tiger, Tiger

I am the tiger,
Free to roam wild,
I am the tiger,
The swiftest avenger,
Blackest of black and colour of sun,
I am the tiger,
Prince of all killers,
Queen of all cats and king of all lies.

But now I'm in danger,
My habitat demolished,
Not free to go wild,
As you hunt for my skin,
I am the tiger,
Deprived of my prey,
As human development,
Threatens my life,
I am the tiger,
Captured and hunted,
My life is destroyed;
All for you humans,
Consumed by greed.

What of my future?
What of my land?
What of my loved ones?
Lost in your 'need'?
What of all cats that roam free in the wild?
Why did you ruin my world for yourself?

I *was* the tiger,
Free to roam wild,
I *was* the tiger,
Prince of all killers.

Rebecca Thorne (12)
Torquay Grammar School for Girls, Torquay

War

I lie there in my trench
My body aching
My arms stiff from holding the gun for so long
A rival steps into view
Into line with my gun
Sweat trickling across my forehead
My finger on the trigger
You spot me
For a brief second your eyes lock onto mine
A brief second is all I need
My finger goes down on the trigger
Click!
Bang!
Shock passes across your features
Before you legs give way and you collapse
I drop my gun
Stunned at my own actions
I didn't think, I just ran
Ran towards you
I knelt down by your side
And stare into your eyes
Your vacant and stained eyes
Your hands lay at your side
Your white and limp hands
Horrified at what I've done
With shaking hands I pick up your pistol
I hear shouting in the far distance
I hold the pistol to my chest
I feel the throbbing of my pulse
I fire, I fall and I die
Yet another body to be added to the ever-growing pile
This is war.

Teagan Feakins (12)
Torquay Grammar School for Girls, Torquay

My Generation

Far away in the distance,
Across the deep, briny sea,
Over the emerald fields,
Is where I'm meant to be.

Instead I'm under the earth,
Where the mud caresses my bones,
Where rain wets my soul,
And where the granite rock moans.

I used to come from Ireland,
I had a soft, southern brogue,
Where I lived with the sky and grass,
And was known as the 'troublesome rogue.'

Oh aye, I rounded the cows and all
And helped harvest the gold hay,
I even slept with the sheep,
With my father from day-to-day.

We had a wee white-washed cottage,
Which was tucked into the heather
And at night the fire danced,
In a room that smelt of leather.

My mother told us stories,
Of monsters and dark nights,
Things that hid in murky lochs,
And children stolen by sprites.

So, while I lie in the soil,
Remembering the golden times,
I sometimes hear children laughing,
And the sound of church bell chimes.

Dani Cole (11)
Torquay Grammar School for Girls, Torquay

Dogs Today

There are so many breeds of dog,
Some run and lope, some merely plod,
Some, a tiny ball of fluff,
Some are big and tall and gruff.

Whippets and greyhounds, born to race,
Salukis and Borzoi, bred for grace,
Chihuahuas and Yorkies, tiny and small,
Golden retrievers, retrieve the ball!

Couch potatoes, sleep and feed,
Like Dalmatians, full of greed,
Some keep going, never stop,
Mutts only halt to roll in slop!

Great Danes are big and tall,
Here are Chihuahuas, smallest of them all,
Any dog, I love them all,
But wait, there is one special mutt . . .

Here is Alfie, my puppy lurcher,
Food guzzler, sofa percher,
He chews and chews everything he can get,
He's licked and loved everyone he has met!

Elizabeth Jones (11)
Torquay Grammar School for Girls, Torquay

Through The Generations

T is for thought which keeps you human
H is for hope that keeps you going
R is for road that you must follow
O is for oceans which you must venture
U is for useful which you should be
G is for giving in which you must take part
H is for honesty in which you must speak

T is for trust in which you must have in others
H is for helpful which you must be
E is for elegance which you must show

G is for grateful which you must be
E is for Earth, which you must protect
N is for nature in which you are surrounded
E is for energy which will keep you going
R is for responsibilities which you will have
A is for action which you should take
T is for triumphant which you will be
I is for intelligence which you have in you
O is for options which you will have
N is for necessary which you are to everyone
S is for sincerity which you must show.

Annabel Strickland (13)
Torquay Grammar School for Girls, Torquay

Turtle's Point Of View

I am a turtle swimming around
Many of us are rarely found,

In the past humans were nice
Bags were thrown, just once or twice,

What has made them change their mind?
Now they're mean, before they were kind,

This generation is mean to me
The amount of bags they throw in the sea,

Bags are thrown into the sea
Humans just don't care about me,

Humans throw them, I can't breathe
It is a crime worse than to thieve,

Killing innocent, sad turtles
Soon you will just kill us all.

Amelia Reid (12)
Torquay Grammar School for Girls, Torquay

My Generation . . .

G irlie chats are the best on our mobile phones
E ating chocolate is a passion
N ew Look is the best place to shop
E xperiencing wicked dreams
R eally loving our friends and family
A cting, singing and dancing we love
T rying new things out
I slands visited around the world
O nly diamonds are a girl's best friend
N atural beauty products are the best.

Emily Jepson (12)
Torquay Grammar School for Girls, Torquay

Magic?

There dwells an alluring valley in Dartmoor,
Captivating rivers trickle downstream,
Gallant rocks loom, creating eerie darkness,
The oak that stands, reverberates with sorrow,
The radiant sun retreats behind the colossal rocks
And by the luminescence of the moon
Silhouettes reveal secrets, so silent,
Nothing: no birds, no sheep, empty silence,
The grass glistens under the morning sun
And suddenly, the world comes to life,
Virgin-blue sky materialises, taking the place of the white moon,
The sparkling water glistens as dragonflies dance in the lilies,
Such beauty,
The birds fly in silent solitude to and from the humble abodes,
The wild horses canter through the marshes
And over the bracken-smothered hills
And again, night descends and the world is plunged into darkness,
The sun will rise again . . .

Charlie Hart (12)
Torquay Grammar School for Girls, Torquay

If I Ruled The World . . .

If I ruled the world
There'd be no such thing as government
No superiors, everyone would be treated as an equal.

No more fights
Wars would be a thing of the past
Of course, world peace would no longer be a dream.

Everyone would have the same rights
Obviously, money wouldn't exist
And then we would all get what we wanted.

If I ruled the world
I'm certain that would all happen
But for now, it's just hopes and dreams . . .

Esther Crompton (11)
Torquay Grammar School for Girls, Torquay

I Wish I Was A Hippy!

I wish I was a hippy
In 1965,
I would have gone to Woodstock
To watch Hendrix play live,
I'd dance around with flowers
And go to San Francisco
And when the decade ended,
I'd change to funk and disco!

Lauren Grace Harper (11)
Torquay Grammar School for Girls, Torquay

Why Don't You Act?

With my own eyes, I saw you,
Dumping litter, not caring where,
You fill me up with landfill,
Now do you really think that's fair?

Oh, many a time I see you,
Flying in a plane,
Breaking down my ozone layer,
To get to France or Spain.

I've heard you time and time again,
Exclaim, 'We need a plan!'
To stop the polar ice caps melting,
Perhaps a driving ban?

But you just stand there, thinking,
Not doing, always thinking,
When can't you see that all the time,
Me, the Earth, I'm shrinking!

Laura Harrison (11)
Torquay Grammar School for Girls, Torquay

Our Generation

Our generation is great,
That's what I think -
And my mate.
There's lots of good food,
Like yummy chocolate -
If you're in the right mood.
And music too,
Like the song, 'Buckle my shoe'.
The technology is good,
But no longer made of wood.
The best is fashion,
It is everyone's passion.
Our generation is great,
That's what I think -
And my mate!

Rosalind Gray (12)
Torquay Grammar School for Girls, Torquay

Farm Dog

The old dog lies on the floor
With his head upon his paws.
He's never in a hurry,
He lazes through the day.

He's a farm dog, he's got lots
Of space to roam
And when he's tired,
He simply comes home.

The old dog lies on the floor,
His eyes so tender and mild,
When he looks at you,
In his eyes, he longs for the wild!

Kirstie Gibling (11)
Torquay Grammar School for Girls, Torquay

Generations

'You won't believe the changes I've seen
All through my lifetime, Jess.'
'Really?' The tiny spider replied,
'I really cannot guess.'

'Well, let me start with Grandpa Bill,
He wasn't always so slow.
A cheeky, agile boy he was,
You'd really never know.

But then he grew and married Pat -
They had two baby boys.
They grew as well and it was fun,
To see such different toys.

Now they have children of their own -
What different lives they lead.
No more conkers or playing cards,
It's Xboxes and Nintendos they need!

The clothes of boys have also changed,
You no longer see a tie,
'Cause now it's jeans, T-shirts and shorts,
It makes poor Grandpa sigh.

Their lives are busy and spent in the car,
They only walk for fun.
But as for me my shell stays on,
I just wait for the summer sun.

Albert the Tortoise - that's my name,
Eighty years I've been around.
The changes I've seen, you wouldn't believe,
The sights, the smells and even the sound.'

'I still don't understand,' sighed Jess,
'About these different relations.'
'Ah, you see - I've heard them talk,
I think they call it generations.'

Laura Powell (12)
Torquay Grammar School for Girls, Torquay

My Generation Poem

We are naughty
We are fun
We have a laugh
With everyone
We love to win
Never lose
Being competitive
Helps our mood
Through our school life
There are ups and downs
Like peer pressure
It makes us frown
But in school
Things are rewarding
Like getting an A
In a subject that's boring
We have our worries
The end of school tests
Scared of failing
And making a mess
But all things aren't bad
Even on your first day
Though you look like a turtle
And being streetwise pay
And although we get stressed
When our homework is rough
We push past it
And bluff that it was tough
So the key to having a blast at school
Is just to have fun and act cool.

Eve Parsons (11)
Torquay Grammar School for Girls, Torquay

Trust

They dumped me on the lonely road,
Then like a streak, they sped;
And the road was so very cold,
That I thought that I was dead:
And as I saw the car, I ran,
Rise, race to catch them up.

You know how silly we dogs are,
I thought it would be fun,
Trying to overtake their car,
I have to run and run,
But as they get faster, faster I went,
I stumbled, sore and spent.

But a kind man found me there,
In the dirt and dust
And he did what he thought fair
And as the days go by, I slowly learn to trust.

I am happy again,
But I never could understand,
Why they left me there, in the dirt and dust
And took away my trust!

Rosie Wood (12)
Torquay Grammar School for Girls, Torquay

Young People

Young people today,
The old wrinklies say.
They look such a mess,
It's the way that they dress.
They only wear black,
With hair down their back.
Got a stud in the ear
And another one here.
I've even seen triples
And rings through the nose.

Their grammar's incorrect
And they show me no respect.
As they walk down the street,
Making passers-by retreat.
They stand in a crowd,
Have music too loud.
Can't talk without swearing,
Or look without glaring.
They don't impress me,
You know, I'm eighty-three.

Tiàna May (12)
Torquay Grammar School for Girls, Torquay

Johnny Depp

He's a world famous actor,
A *huge* movie star,
The love of my life
And he plays the guitar.

His film career,
It's a *big* success,
Even in Edward;
When he had to wear a dress!

Pirates of the Caribbean,
This film has to be one of the best!
Captain Jack Sparrow,
Who *could* lose interest?

This man should rule the world!
He *totally, totally* rocks!
I love him to bits,
Even if he *does* wear smelly socks!

Brittany Brown (11)
Torquay Grammar School for Girls, Torquay

Interpretation

This is an interpretation,
One made up by me.
It's my meaning of friendship,
A ship ne'er sailed the sea.

Friendship's like a bouncy ball,
As far as I can tell.
Flying up high and then down low,
According to how it fell.

Friends and their moods go up and down,
For that is how it is.
You just have to accept it,
So don't get in a tizz.

This is an interpretation,
One made up by me.
It's my meaning of friendship,
A ship ne'er sailed the sea.

Helen Gillard (12)
Torquay Grammar School for Girls, Torquay

The World Could Be . . .

I look out my window
And stare at the sea,
I think about the lives,
Of everyone, but me.
I think of the world
And how it could be,
But that will not happen,
Not even maybe.

The world could be peaceful,
The world could be safe,
But I know that it won't
Even come close.

The world at the moment,
Is losing control,
As people are using,
Too much of the coal.
They also are using,
Some more precious stuff,
Like copper and steel,
It's turning the world rough.

The world could be peaceful,
The world could be safe,
But I know that it won't,
Even come close.

Jessica Knapman (11)
Torquay Grammar School for Girls, Torquay

Who Am I?

The emos and goths,
The rockers and the skater,
The chavs and the boffs
And our world, the creator.

So, am I a chav or a rocker?
An emo or a boff?
I know one thing for sure,
I'm definitely not a goth.

I have hair like an emo,
I think like a boff,
I act like a rocker,
But nothing like a goth.

I think I'll be a rocker
And play on my guitar,
So what, I'm not an emo,
That steals my mother's car.

A rocker isn't me,
Neither an emo nor a chav,
Just an old saying from my family,
I am who I am.

Brogan Ferrol (11)
Torquay Grammar School for Girls, Torquay

I Am Not Who You Think I Am . . .

I am 14, female
I'm pretty - blonde, blue eyes
I'm popular
I have hundreds of friends on Facebook
I'm cool
I wear awesome clothes
River Island, Topshop
I love music
Paramore, My Chemical Romance
I love films
Orlando Bloom
I love coffee
Starbucks
I love to sit and chat
In my room
Alone
My wife
And children downstairs
I am 41, male

I am not who you think I am.

Tilly Ross (12)
Torquay Grammar School for Girls, Torquay

If I Ruled The World

If I ruled the world
Nobody would be sad
And everything on the Earth
Would be completely mad.
For breakfast we'd eat chocolate cake
And our mum would say,
'Well done my lovely children,
That's one of your five-a-day!'
Everyone would dye their hair
Pink, purple, green or red
And lessons would take place
From the comfort of your bed.
Teachers would give out cash
For work that was done well.
You'd never have to be quiet
And you could shout and yell!
If I ruled the world
Nobody would be sad
And all the things on the planet
Would be completely mad!

Lucy Kember (13)
Torquay Grammar School for Girls, Torquay

If I Could Change The World

If I could change the world,
I'll tell you what I'd do,
To make it a better place,
For the future me and you.

I'd end all world poverty,
I'd help all those in need,
I'd give them food and shelter
And help them plant the seed.

I'd stop global warming,
I'd make everyone aware,
Of the damage we are doing,
When we pollute the air.

I'd get rid of discrimination,
Whether gender, creed or race,
I'd make equal opportunities,
To put a smile on every face.

I would then bring world peace,
To stop the wars and fighting,
As we are all the same,
It's a new candle we'll be lighting.

'Know your history,' said Roosevelt,
'So you can influence and alter,
The future of your nation,
A road on which you must not falter.'

If I could change the world,
I'll tell you what I'd do,
To make it a better place,
For the future me and you.

Isabelle Walford (12)
Torquay Grammar School for Girls, Torquay

Make The Most Of It!

Life is short,
Life is fun,
Life is a game,
That's never been won!

Life is boring,
Life is sad,
Life is painful,
It can drive you mad!

Life is happy,
Life is full,
Life is great,
But be careful!

Life is tiring,
Life is work,
Life never stops,
But it has its perks!

Life is peaceful,
Life is play,
Life is rest,
But not every day!

Life is hard,
Don't you quit,
Life doesn't last,
So make the most of it!

Constance Collier-Qureshy (12)
Torquay Grammar School for Girls, Torquay

Mermaid Rock

The ferocious waves,
Of the sapphire sea,
Crash against the shore
And spray all over me.

As I step through the sand,
I feel an urge to go,
Into the deep blue ocean
And see the coral grow.

While swimming through the water,
I make a magical wish,
To see the snail and the seahorse,
The crab and the starfish.

I am approaching a rock,
Where I had recently played
And I see something strange,
Not a girl, but a mermaid.

Harriet Cox (11)
Torquay Grammar School for Girls, Torquay

My Day At School

I'm travelling to school,
It's raining like a pool.
There's the snow,
It's white below.
Here comes the bus,
The pupils rush.
As the bells chime,
The children rhyme.
First lessons start,
The students dart.
The sound of chatter,
Makes the building shatter.
My tummy rumbles,
As the food tumbles.
As the end of the day draws nearer,
The sofa becomes clearer.
I hope you like my poem,
It's about my generation.

Zoe Gluning (12)
Torquay Grammar School for Girls, Torquay

Twelve

I look in the mirror
And what do I see?
I see myself looking at me.

I look in the mirror
Deep in my eyes
And find myself wondering
What, in the future, lies?

I look in the mirror
With dreams in my mind
Hoping all my dreams and wishes
I will definitely find.

I smile in the mirror
And realise at this hour
I do not need to worry
As I am still a young flower -

Twelve.

Chloe Scott-Perkins (12)
Torquay Grammar School for Girls, Torquay

What Is Life?

Life is full of choices
And many different voices

Life is full of surprises,
In many different sizes

Life is full of emotions,
Love, passion and devotion

Life is full of disappointments,
That come with many ointments

Life is full of glory,
Always with a story

Life is full of crime,
But heals over time

Yet life still goes on,
You have got to move on.

Rebecca Squire (12)
Torquay Grammar School for Girls, Torquay

Deep In The Jungle
(A warning to prospective predators of the human species!)

The scorching, sticky blackness,
Lay thick and heavy like tar,
Swallowing me further and further,
Deep in the jungle

Treacherous swaying vines,
Grabbed, choked and strangled,
An unfortunate canopy of towering trees,
Deep in the jungle

The thorny, spiky twigs and leaves,
Enshrouded and curled around my bare feet,
More and more at each heart-stopping step,
Deep in the jungle

Was I lost? Who knows?
As all of the blood in my veins froze to ice,
When I sensed I was being followed, *watched*,
Deep in the jungle

Was it bloodthirsty leopards ready to pounce?
Or fat, life-squeezing snakes?
In the dead of night, anything could be lurking,
Deep in the jungle

Without warning, *it* leapt out, piercing my throat,
What was it? I'll never, ever know,
For here I will lie, bloody and dead forever,
Deep in the jungle!

Sophie Biddick (12)
Torquay Grammar School for Girls, Torquay

Another School Day

I woke up gloomy and tired
Last night I stayed up late
But there's no time for breakfast
I've hardly touched my plate

I must be at the bus stop
Where the seats are lined with grime
But I don't care, I must be there
To get to school on time

I enter the noisy classroom
I stand so calm and quiet
But not everything is tranquillity
The air is a whirlpool of riot

I've finally finished three lessons
Geography, English and French
Hooray! It's time for lunch now
I'll eat it on the bench

It's nearly the end of the school day
Can't wait to get home and lie down
I say bye to my friends and get on the bus
On a seat that is dirty and brown

I'm home at last, where I can relax
But just as I think I can rest
I realise I've got homework to do
Why is homework such a pest?

So, I stayed up till ten last night
Like many days before
School is sometimes such a nuisance
But sometimes . . .

I wish there could be more!

Hayley Norman (12)
Torquay Grammar School for Girls, Torquay

I Looked Out Over The World

I looked out over the world today
And saw the sky so grey,
I felt the raindrops on my skin,
That fall with every day.

I watched the cars go driving by,
The aeroplanes in the air,
I saw the boats, the trains, the fumes
And said, 'This isn't fair.'

I looked out over the world today
And in my mind I saw,
The monkeys, snakes and canopies,
That aren't there anymore.

But why? I thought, *why cut them down?*
We need them for the world!
And I missed the rainforests, green and bright,
With their leaves, so large and curled.

I looked out over the world today
And polar bears I saw,
The ice and snow all melted
And the bears fell to the floor.

The glaciers began to melt,
The North Pole disappeared,
Britain was flooded and homes were lost,
Just the way we feared.

I looked out over the world today
And thought, *what have we done?*
I looked out over the world today
With tears in my eyes.

Emily Watton (12)
Torquay Grammar School for Girls, Torquay

If I Ruled The World

If I ruled the world
Everything would be free
All the boys and girls
Running round with glee.

If I ruled the world
People wouldn't pay tax
A sigh of relief to all parents
They can sit down and relax.

If I ruled the world
Money would grow on trees
Buy anything with endless money
The poor, my rule would please.

If I ruled the world,
Sport would be my priority,
Tennis, rugby, football, swimming
Those who didn't play would be a minority.

If I ruled the world
Family would come first
It may already come the top
But families' bubbles wouldn't burst.

The truth is a hard thing
I will never get my dream
It is a nice thought though
But no one rules the world, so harsh that may seem.

Emily Plester (12)
Torquay Grammar School for Girls, Torquay

The Meaning Of Life

Why are we here?
To laugh,
To live
And even die?

What is the point?
To help,
To love
And even fight?

How much longer?
With poverty
And death?
Who knows?

Demi Butcher (13)
Torquay Grammar School for Girls, Torquay

My Generation

It's not very safe to go out at night,
Hooligans and thieves doing what they shouldn't be,
It's not very safe to go out at night,
Con men and fraudsters using their sly trickery,
It's not very safe to go out at night,
Because you could get one big fright!

It's safe to go out in the day,
To go on down to the amusement arcade,
It's safe to go out in the day,
To meet up with friends in town,
It's safe to go out in the day,
As hooligans and thieves hide away!

Livvy Davidson (12)
Torquay Grammar School for Girls, Torquay

If I Ruled The World

If I ruled the world
Everything would be free
All the boys and girls
Running round with glee.

If I ruled the world
People wouldn't pay tax
A sigh of relief to all parents
They can sit down and relax.

If I ruled the world
Money would grow on trees
Buy anything with endless money
The poor, my rule would please.

If I ruled the world,
Sport would be my priority,
Tennis, rugby, football, swimming
Those who didn't play would be a minority.

If I ruled the world
Family would come first
It may already come the top
But families' bubbles wouldn't burst.

The truth is a hard thing
I will never get my dream
It is a nice thought though
But no one rules the world, so harsh that may seem.

Emily Plester (12)
Torquay Grammar School for Girls, Torquay

The Meaning Of Life

Why are we here?
To laugh,
To live
And even die?

What is the point?
To help,
To love
And even fight?

How much longer?
With poverty
And death?
Who knows?

Demi Butcher (13)
Torquay Grammar School for Girls, Torquay

My Generation

It's not very safe to go out at night,
Hooligans and thieves doing what they shouldn't be,
It's not very safe to go out at night,
Con men and fraudsters using their sly trickery,
It's not very safe to go out at night,
Because you could get one big fright!

It's safe to go out in the day,
To go on down to the amusement arcade,
It's safe to go out in the day,
To meet up with friends in town,
It's safe to go out in the day,
As hooligans and thieves hide away!

Livvy Davidson (12)
Torquay Grammar School for Girls, Torquay

My Generation

M e and
Y ou

G rabbing chances
E nduring glances
N ever stopping
E ndless shopping
R acking brains
A voiding pains
T ackling fears
I ncluding peers
O penly giving
N ow we're living!

Sukayna Zayer (12)
Torquay Grammar School for Girls, Torquay

Meaning Of Life

To some, life means a flower,
A new start, new beginning.
To others, life means power,
Money and possessions.

To some, life means a dove,
Looking beautiful and perfect.
To others, life means true love,
To share your heart and soul.

To some, life means kindness,
Joy and happiness to others.
To others, it means sadness,
Alone, hiding from this world.

Chloe Murthwaite (13)
Torquay Grammar School for Girls, Torquay

Falling

What you see is what you get,
So don't read between the lines.
This world's been left in serious debt
And now we see the signs.
You see it's not from pounds, Euros or cents,
But love and health and care.
The planet's been plagued with bumps and dents
And has given us quite a scare.
It's lacking in things that help the world,
But is swamped with pollution and war.
Around and around it has been whirled,
In an everlasting tour.
A cycle of damage and painful results,
To add to an age of despair.
Now we've given the world some noticeable faults,
It's suffered some wear and tear.
It's time to stop this constant falling,
Into the abyss.
Open that parachute with a spring,
But it's falling that we'll miss.
Open it up before it's too late,
Make sure you don't hit the ground.
Slow down the falling rate,
But just don't make a sound.

Catherine Seymour (13)
Torquay Grammar School for Girls, Torquay

A Refugee Story

I am an outcast, on my own,
No one to hold me, all alone,
I see only torture and fear,
No one will spare me money and made it clear,
They stamp on me, spit on my cheek,
My life is miserable, my life is bleak,
'But how can you live?' You might say,
Hope only keeps us going each and every day,
The thought that something will come real soon,
As we stare at the sky, stars and moon,
Through my eyes, I see only emptiness and pain,
I walk in the mud and sleep in the rain,
We are not excepted, for I am a refugee,
All of us are neglected, including me,
My grandpa once said, 'Stand on your own,'
How can I do that, with moan after moan?
My daughter, barely three,
Knows none of compassion or commiseration,
The rest are gone to a faraway land,
My name is Sandy Slater and here I stand.

Philippa Adams (13)
Torquay Grammar School for Girls, Torquay

The Flock

Through my eyes,
As I watch,
From the skies,
The world is approaching its demise.

Through my heart,
My love for her,
A tight bond,
It's growing stronger.

Through my ears,
As I'm blind,
No longer I see,
The future kind.

Through my touch,
I know who's been there,
My love for computers,
Do I talk too much?

Through my dreams,
The sky's a gloom,
Erasers coming,
To complete our doom.

Through my mind,
I hear their thoughts,
Some good, some bad,
I should withdraw.

This is our flock,
We have wings, you know,
We have to stop it,
Or the world will blow.

Lucy Ricketts (11)
Torquay Grammar School for Girls, Torquay

Life, But Why?

Why were humans put here?
My teeth grind like a knife,
My head buzzes over and over,
To discover the meaning of life.

Are we here to protect?
To tell the world the way,
Were we made to help,
Or just to pass the day?

Were animals meant to be caged?
Was it always meant to be?
I fear not, because of what,
I dread and what I see.

The world is a terrible mess,
I look and I feel sad,
The humans just leave it,
To slowly go bad.

Life was never meant for this,
We have to change our ways,
If we don't, we'll slowly,
Be numbering our days.

But there is hope,
Through all this strife,
If we change the world,
We turn around life.

Isabelle Sach (13)
Torquay Grammar School for Girls, Torquay

The World - My Generation

M is for my world
   It changes each step I take
Y is for your world
   It's your responsibility
G is for great world
   Without the world we wouldn't be here
E is for everyone's world
   Helping to save our planet
N is for the natural world
   The forests, the trees and the busy bees
E is for expanding world
   Watch the population rise
R is for revolutionary world
   Fight for what is right
A is for active world
   Plenty of sports for us to try
T is for technology world
   The fun and knowledge from our new-found world
I is for an international world
   The cultures have come together
O is for our world
   Our world is in our hands
N is for new world
   Creating new history for the next generation!

Courtney Beth Clarke (11)
Torquay Grammar School for Girls, Torquay

Life, But Why?

Why were humans put here?
My teeth grind like a knife,
My head buzzes over and over,
To discover the meaning of life.

Are we here to protect?
To tell the world the way,
Were we made to help,
Or just to pass the day?

Were animals meant to be caged?
Was it always meant to be?
I fear not, because of what,
I dread and what I see.

The world is a terrible mess,
I look and I feel sad,
The humans just leave it,
To slowly go bad.

Life was never meant for this,
We have to change our ways,
If we don't, we'll slowly,
Be numbering our days.

But there is hope,
Through all this strife,
If we change the world,
We turn around life.

Isabelle Sach (13)
Torquay Grammar School for Girls, Torquay

The World - My Generation

M is for my world
   It changes each step I take
Y is for your world
   It's your responsibility
G is for great world
   Without the world we wouldn't be here
E is for everyone's world
   Helping to save our planet
N is for the natural world
   The forests, the trees and the busy bees
E is for expanding world
   Watch the population rise
R is for revolutionary world
   Fight for what is right
A is for active world
   Plenty of sports for us to try
T is for technology world
   The fun and knowledge from our new-found world
I is for an international world
   The cultures have come together
O is for our world
   Our world is in our hands
N is for new world
   Creating new history for the next generation!

Courtney Beth Clarke (11)
Torquay Grammar School for Girls, Torquay

I'm Just Me

I sit, I watch, I wait, I stare
While all the others whisper and glare
And I can't help just being me
So why can't everyone simply see
I'm the same as them, but do they even care?

Though I might have a helper, a teacher, a friend
It really doesn't mean I've gone round the bend
Who cares if I can't talk, I'll use my hands; why not?
I have different gifts to what you've got
All I ask of you, is for your help, be a teacher, be a friend.

Amy Britton (11)
Torquay Grammar School for Girls, Torquay

Why Are We Here?

Why are we here?
People live,
People die,
Same old story.

But for how much longer?
With poverty
And war,
You might well ask.

And what do we do?
Nothing,
We let it happen,
We close off our hearts.

So, why are we here?
Why do people live?
Why do people die?
Is it the same old story?

Emma Pottle (13)
Torquay Grammar School for Girls, Torquay

The World's Dying Out

I am the grass of the world around you,
Muddy and not so fresh
For I am the Earth and I'm treated badly,
By all this human flesh.

There's no more time,
The world's dying out
There's no more time,
No time to shout out.

The trees are dead,
The fields are brown
The world is turning,
Upside down.

There's no more time,
The world's dying out
There's no more time,
No time to shout out.

Ashleigh Catherine Rawlings (11)
Torquay Grammar School for Girls, Torquay

River To Sea

I gush over rocks, grinding them down,
I lead the fish to sea,
I used to run through fields and valleys,
But now I run past roads and buildings cut my root,
I cry to the land, try to spread my wings, but Man controls me,
Man hears me, but doesn't listen,
Man pollutes me and changes me,
I cry.

Vicky Hall (13)
Truro High School for Girls, Truro

Why?

Why do stars look so happy?
They shine and twinkle in the sky
They never seem to falter, they never seem to cry.

Why does the sun seem so bright?
It shimmers a pale gold
It never loses it lustre, it never goes cold.

Why do flowers blossom?
They bring joy to young and old
They never seem to wilt, they never seem to mould.

How can anything be cheerful?
Have a spring in their step
No one will ever know the tale I've kept
Or how much I've ever wept.

Kelly Bowden (13)
Truro High School for Girls, Truro

His World

A newborn baby lies outside
His tiny little eyes not yet able to open
To see the world and its highs
To see the world he would grow into

However, when his eyelids begin to stir
When his eyes begin to see
The world that once began so great
Was now all grey and buildings towered above the sky.

Was this the world that he deserved to see?
Was this the world that should have been?
Was this the world that we all love?
Or do we wish it was like it used to be?

Anna Phillips (12)
Truro High School for Girls, Truro

My Generation

My generation is different to yours,
Your generation is full of old bores.

Your generation likes biscuits and tea,
My generation prefers KFC.

My generation likes Topshop and Claire's,
Your generation just falls down the stairs.

Your generation goes on about school,
My generation is funky and cool.

My generation likes make-up, it's ace,
Your generation say, 'What's on your face?'

Your generation has clothes with no passion,
My generation is all about fashion.

My generation will start a new trend,
When your generation has come to an end.

Jade Bowmer (12)
Truro High School for Girls, Truro

Changed

My soul is bleeding,
His heart is leaving,
Sadness of life,
Sorrow of days,
He has changed me.
He has gone,
I will stay,
Forever is life,
The pain of days,
Changed forever,
Trapped forever.

Tippi Jensen (13)
Truro High School for Girls, Truro

Trapped: A Fox Cub's Tale

Mother's gone,
Father left,
Everything ruined,
Everything dead,

They came with hounds,
They came with horses,
It happened so fast,
They tracked us down,
So close to the burrow,
Not close enough,
They got her,

I am all alone,
There is no way out,
I can't escape,
I am dead.

Lauren Bose (12)
Truro High School for Girls, Truro

Misunderstood

My generation, we skate and have fun,
My generation does sport and runs.
My generation wears make-up around their eyes,
My generation always asks why?
My generation listens to rock,
My generations can't live without a door lock.
My generation is misunderstood,
My generation has fun like it should.

Danielle Blackburn (12)
Truro High School for Girls, Truro

Changes

Nowadays hoodies in the streets
Scaring everyone that passes by
Shouting, scaring
It never used to be like this
There used to be hopscotch in the main street
Now there is just graffiti

Sad it is
Everyone gloomy
It shouldn't be like this
This used to be a happy street
Everyone smiling, having fun
Not caring what you wore
Why has it changed so much?

Where I used to play
Is now a block of flats
Buildings, cars, factories
Everywhere I look
Sadness upon people
Why is the world so strict nowadays?

Everywhere I look, nothing the same
Traffic, violence and building sites
It never used to be like this
Everyone said, 'Hi!'
Not give people the look
Why did it change so much?

Katie Slater (13)
Truro High School for Girls, Truro

The Racehorse

I could smell the hay that should be mine,
I could still taste the bit in my mouth,
I could still feel the saddle on my back,
I could see nothing, but the inside of my stable,
I could hear the celebrations of another horse's win.

That race had been tiring,
I had tried my best,
I had lost by a mile,
My owner had been angry with me,
I had been sent to this tiny, dark stable.

This had been my last chance,
If I lost this one, it would be over,
My legs were weak,
I fell to the floor,
I shut my eyes.

I tried to cry out,
No one heard me,
My call was too feeble,
I tried to weep,
But all my tears were gone.

I struggled to my feet,
But only fell again,
There was no one there to help me,
I gave in to the darkness,
That night the darkness had consumed another of its victims.

Rosie Curry (13)
Truro High School for Girls, Truro

Headache

I had a headache today
My friends led me astray
Not having fun anymore
Shattered on the floor
Like a broken ashtray.

I have a headache tonight
It's not helpful in my plight
To succeed, I have to, there's no choice
I'm led to believe I have a voice
But I don't, there is no fight.

I'll have a headache tomorrow
And a temperature is bound to follow
Some make-up and a kettle
Pretend I cannot settle
I don't want to go to school tomorrow.

Amy Mayne (16) & Holly Doick (17)
Twynham School, Christchurch

Why Me?

I was taken from my family at birth
Left cold and lonely in the spotlight
Caged young, for what purpose?
Night is dark and scary
As the moonlight hits my eyes
White coats hung up neatly
Blue gloves spread out everywhere
Sharp metal objects jab me
Like terrifying lightning
The selfish people who don't take any notice
Will feel guilty when they find out my feelings
I walk around the cold metal cage
Looking for a way out
To flee from this nightmare I am having
There is no freedom for me.

Elieze Hinchcliffe (11)
Twynham School, Christchurch

My Dog, Penny

I took my dog for a walk
And then, she started to talk,
The stress was starting to show,
But then she stopped and said, 'No.'

When we got home, she wanted a rest,
In a way she'd had a running test,
All of a sudden, she started to snore,
A terrible noise, we had to ignore.

Ten hours later, she finally awakes,
She wanted to go out, for goodness sake!
At the door, she began to bark,
Showing her teeth, a bit like a shark.

Some would believe a bulldog is ugly,
But to us she is truly lovely,
Penny the bulldog is my very best friend
And now this poem must come to an end.

William Broomfield (12)
Twynham School, Christchurch

My Poem

Oh no! I don't know what to write
I have been up thinking all of the night
If the homework is not complete
I will have a detention for the rest of the week!
I could say I sent it into the competition . . .
But my teacher would knock me into submission!
Maybe I should just give up . . .
But if I couldn't finish it, it would really suck!
I could say the dog ate . . .
But she would tell me to hand it in late!
Or I could finish it now
And save myself a row!

Callum Mercer (12)
Twynham School, Christchurch

School

You might think school is nice
Soppy teachers serve beans and rice
But the school I go to, is so *not* cool
No fun sports, no swimming pool!

Life's unfair, why not be dead?
Cos I do lines for scratching my head
I get told off for looking sad
When you can't blame me for the day I've had!

Now life is hard and my teachers kick
Or beat me with a wooden stick
But I forget my scars and all
When I'm being crushed against the wall!

All day long, it's just work
Behind each corner, teachers may lurk
Ready, waiting to smack you bad
To make you squeal and make you sad!

Every time a teacher's near
They drag you along by the ear
I run away, duck and dive
If they want you, you'd better *hide!*

I tell my mum, I tell my dad
About the terrible day I've had
But they won't take one word in
I don't think I'll ever win!

Jerome Parramore (12)
Twynham School, Christchurch

My Dog, Penny

I took my dog for a walk
And then, she started to talk,
The stress was starting to show,
But then she stopped and said, 'No.'

When we got home, she wanted a rest,
In a way she'd had a running test,
All of a sudden, she started to snore,
A terrible noise, we had to ignore.

Ten hours later, she finally awakes,
She wanted to go out, for goodness sake!
At the door, she began to bark,
Showing her teeth, a bit like a shark.

Some would believe a bulldog is ugly,
But to us she is truly lovely,
Penny the bulldog is my very best friend
And now this poem must come to an end.

William Broomfield (12)
Twynham School, Christchurch

My Poem

Oh no! I don't know what to write
I have been up thinking all of the night
If the homework is not complete
I will have a detention for the rest of the week!
I could say I sent it into the competition . . .
But my teacher would knock me into submission!
Maybe I should just give up . . .
But if I couldn't finish it, it would really suck!
I could say the dog ate . . .
But she would tell me to hand it in late!
Or I could finish it now
And save myself a row!

Callum Mercer (12)
Twynham School, Christchurch

School

You might think school is nice
Soppy teachers serve beans and rice
But the school I go to, is so *not* cool
No fun sports, no swimming pool!

Life's unfair, why not be dead?
Cos I do lines for scratching my head
I get told off for looking sad
When you can't blame me for the day I've had!

Now life is hard and my teachers kick
Or beat me with a wooden stick
But I forget my scars and all
When I'm being crushed against the wall!

All day long, it's just work
Behind each corner, teachers may lurk
Ready, waiting to smack you bad
To make you squeal and make you sad!

Every time a teacher's near
They drag you along by the ear
I run away, duck and dive
If they want you, you'd better *hide!*

I tell my mum, I tell my dad
About the terrible day I've had
But they won't take one word in
I don't think I'll ever win!

Jerome Parramore (12)
Twynham School, Christchurch

Nosferatu

He rose from the grave,
With a bloodcurdling cry,
He opened his wings and began to fly,
Red eyes, on a white face,
He started flapping and picked up pace,
All of a sudden, he started to slow,
A neck was bitten and blood started to flow,
This was the first victim of the night,
Once again, he started his flight,
He looked hard for his second catch,
This one was more of a match,
They fought for a while,
Till the man fell in a pile,
He dived at the man gracefully,
Finished him off silently,
Once again he looked for prey,
The sun was coming, so was day,
There she was, the third and last,
This one he would devour fast,
He moved closer, 'No!'
'No more will the blood flow!'
He saw nought but the dark,
Heard nought but the lark!
The morning was here,
Yes, the end was near,
A stake was put through his heart,
But alas, this creature had no heart,
The sun shone light,
No more would this creature bite,
Bright, pure, white light.

Scott Couldridge (14)
Twynham School, Christchurch

A New Friend

I woke up today, all sunny and bright
But then my owner went out of my sight
I can't believe they left me here to stay
While they have fun on holiday!
Who is that coming down the stairs?
Must be my owner's friend, at least someone cares!
I'm so glad to see her, she looks very kind
She doesn't give me treats, but I don't mind
I sit by the door, hoping for a run
Will she take a ball? That would be fun!
We've finished our walk, we're now back at home
Look what she's got me! A big, juicy bone!
Being left at home is not so bad
My owners are back soon and I am glad.

Seana Morrison (12)
Twynham School, Christchurch

Out In The Cold

I am a dog,
Lost and cold,
I am going to die,
Though I'm not very old,
My owner has left me,
He's not coming back,
I think he is angry,
He's been given the sack,
I hear a door opening,
My name has been called,
My owner comes running,
He had me fooled,
He told me he did care,
He just needed some space,
He really did love me,
I was impossible to replace.

Danielle Palombo (12)
Twynham School, Christchurch

What Can I Hear? What Can I See?

What can I hear? What can I see?
That little object by my knee,
Is it a snail? Is it a slug?
I think it might be a big scary bug!

What can I hear? What can I see?
That little object running away from me,
Is it my dog? Is it my cat?
I think it might be a small squeaky rat!

What can I hear? What can I see?
That big object that's standing next to me,
Is it my sister? Is it my mother?
I think it might be my annoying big brother!

What can I hear? What can I see?
That big object in front of me,
Is it a window? Is it a tree?
I think it might just be *me!*

Ella Somers (12)
Twynham School, Christchurch

Teachers!

Teachers are mean
Teachers are bad
Sometimes they make me feel really sad

They give out homework
Which can be really hard
Sometimes it might be to design a card

Some of them can shout
When you ask them a question
That's only in some of my lessons

Teachers can be sporty
Others can be warty
This shall show you what your teachers are like.

Ashley Reedman (12)
Twynham School, Christchurch

The Cornwall Crush

As I awake,
The light shines in,
The tweets and the whistles,
As the morning birds sing,

I open the curtains,
The sun bursts through,
It hits like an ocean,
That fills up the room,

A cup of tea greets me,
With a hug and a kiss,
My breakfast awaits,
As the sausages hiss,

The gravel path crunches,
Underneath my feet,
The sea is in sight,
As my hand and board meet,

The coldness of the sea,
As it touches my feet,
The board is beneath me,
Like a soft safety sheet,

I turn to the left,
As I pick up speed,
Chased by the whitewash,
But I'm in the lead,

I could do this all day,
Until the sun is asleep,
For I know the next day,
The sun and I will meet.

Kelly Haynes (11)
Twynham School, Christchurch

The Gale

It was on a Monday
When a gale came.

As the children were playing
It started to heavily rain.

The grass and bushes were wet
As well as the school pet.

All of the litter was blowing
But the children thought it was snowing.

They thought it would never end
When the trees started to bend.

It was then when they heard the thunder
They started to wonder
If they were going to go home in the thunder.

Just at that moment, the teacher said
'We can't get home, so make a bed.'

It was early the next morning, the gale stopped
The children woke up and their eyes popped.

When they got home, the gale started again
So at school, all the children had to make beds again.

Jordan Trellis (11)
Twynham School, Christchurch

Shattered

A land of terror, hunger and pain,
From this war, what do we gain?
Death, pain, hunger and fear,
We cry out, yet no one hears.

Houses left abandoned, people left alone,
Only rage and fear are now left to show.

Children's screams,
Shattered dreams,
Separation, tears, cruel laughter that sears,
Marching back and forth, day and night,
What is the reason for this fight?

Isolation, lonely cells, friends gone forever,
Loss, misery, the pain stays forever.

Who can say what will happen?
Not us, we only sit and wait,
Dying for freedom, fresh air and laughter,
The end might be early, it might be late.

Hiding, constant threats of death and being found,
It could be a look, a movement, a sound.

Arresting innocent people,
Thrown into jail,
Pain thrown into every heart,
Sharp as a nail.

Escaping the camps, death as punishment,
Screams of fear and pain, is there judgement?

Lives were lost, but time goes on,
No one will be forgotten,
Mother, father, daughter or son.

At the end of the tunnel, there is a glimmer of light,
After all these wars, we now know not to fight.

Now I must say, all is said, all is done,
The war was lost, the war was won
And all I have said, please keep it in your head
And now, my dear reader, the last thing . . .

The end!

Ruby Caitlin McMahon (11)
Twynham School, Christchurch

Meaning Of Life

I always wondered why we are here,
To live or die?
To work or play?
To smile or cry?

Who am I?
What do I stand for?
Do I like adventures
Or a nice night in?
Summer or winter?
Autumn or spring?

What makes me, me?
Is it the colour of my skin
Or the colour of my eyes?
Is it how I look
Or what goes on inside?

I've always wanted to know why I am me
But I'd have nothing to wonder about
If that secret was free
The world is such a big place
Compared to it, I'm small
The world has so many secrets
It's impossible to know them all!

Georgia Smith & Lauren Fry (14)
Twynham School, Christchurch

Match Abuse

I get hit around every day,
Back and forth, to and fro,
I dare not fray,
When I hit the strings, I feel so low.

Got over the net, hit the ground,
I knew it was going to happen,
I hate that pounding sound,
Wilson's a lethal weapon!

When he hits an ace,
My job is now done,
I have no face,
But my journey's just begun.

Elizabeth Coombes (13) & Katie Mitchell (14)
Twynham School, Christchurch

It's A Twin Thing

A twin is the best friend you could ever know,
Being together, wherever you go.
Sharing ideas and sharing thoughts,
Crazy ideas of all sorts.
Blonde hair, blue eyes,
Same colour as the skies.
What we are doing, always funny,
Even if we lose pocket money.
Having fun throughout the day,
Doing everything our way.
Sharing a room when we were small,
It was really cool.
Helping each other with homework and stuff,
Even if the job is hard and tough.
This poem is just to say,
Twins are really OK!

Holly Du Cros (12)
Twynham School, Christchurch

My Animal Poem

M ost animals are gorgeous, all fluffy and cute
Y et people don't think this when they think of a newt

A n eagle's so graceful, soaring in the sky
N obody knows what it's like to fly
I love lions who are scary, but proud
M onkeys are cheeky and can be incredibly loud
A nd alligators too can be quite snappy
L aughing hyenas always seem happy

P eople forget fish have feelings too
O rcas don't like being kept in a zoo
E ven though I think we should show them all care
M y favourite's the tiger, because it's so rare.

Sophie Duffell (12)
Twynham School, Christchurch

The Misunderstood Generation

We're who we are,
Not who you want us to be,
But understand this,
We're not who you see.

Guns and knives,
It's all an illusion,
The world's youth today,
Surrounded by confusion.

We hang around in gangs,
For fun, not fights,
So tell me this now,
Why do we keep you up at night?

We're who we are,
Not who you want us to be,
But understand this,
We're not who you see.

Georgina Farmer (13)
Twynham School, Christchurch

Mornings

I wake up in the morning
Tired and still yawning
Knowing I've got school this day
I shrink down into my duvet

In my bed, it feels so warm
Surely it can't yet be dawn?
But Dad is singing in the shower
Oh no, I haven't even got an hour!

Mum is knocking at my door
I close my eyes, pretend to snore
'Hurry kids, or you'll be late
I really don't have time to wait!'

My uniform is on my bed
These minutes are the ones I dread
I get dressed in slow motion
Not one bit of determination

I dash to brush my teeth and hair
Search for the blazer I have to wear
I want to have a cup of tea
But Dad is shouting out to me

Now he's beeping in his car
I cannot walk, it is too far
No choice, I simply have to go
Morning's not my favourite time, you know!

Amber Porter (11)
Twynham School, Christchurch

The Beautiful Creature

A creature approached me, such a beautiful thing
It fluttered past with each delicate wing
It fluttered from rose to rose
Then fluttered past my nose
I waited
It waited
I stood up
It panicked
I waited
It fluttered
I waited
It flew high
Soaring to the sky
The wings glowed in the sun's ray
'What a beautiful creature,' I wished to say
It flew to a tree
Where I couldn't see
I waited
It kept out of sight
I moved
It flew high
Soaring to the sky
It landed on my head
It flew over the fence
'Goodbye, My Butterfly!'

Zoë Seabourne (11)
Twynham School, Christchurch

Imagination

'Breathe,' the girl whispered
And blew into the unicorn's feathers,
The unicorn grew to full size,
Its coat as tough as leather.

The patchwork pony, the fairy too,
They burst into life, flying wildly about,
The girl looked on with joy,
Her animals alive, without a doubt.

Wild stag, deer and sheep,
They all came alive in front of her eyes,
Magically moving,
Growing in size.

Suddenly, the sunlight poured in,
It forced its way inside the room,
The animals shrunk back down to size,
They fell to the floor with an almighty boom.

They lay helplessly on the floor,
As lifeless as could be,
For the animals were rare,
For only some to see.

The little girl stared at the small, stuffed toys,
That lay on the floor; their words not spoken,
She rearranged them, back on her bed,
Her eyes dazzled, but the spell was broken.

Laura Maw (13)
Twynham School, Christchurch

What I Am!

I'm neither happy nor sad,
But I often feel quite bad,
But when I cry,
I feel like I want to die.

When I hurt my mates,
It's not all that great,
But when they're happy,
I feel very happy.

War is good,
War is bad,
But when people die,
I feel quite sad.

When I wake up every day,
All my worries go away,
But when it rains,
I cry again.

Love comes from all my hate,
But when it comes back,
I know I'm too late,
But when I'm angry I'm like a fire.

But when I smile,
I wait a while,
For a small breeze,
To blow me away.

Sarah Bishop (13) & Shannon Vare (14)
Twynham School, Christchurch

Newborn Baby

I am a newborn baby, so cute, so small,
People coo and fuss over me, but I'm not bothered at all,
I get passed to visitors like a parcel wrapped up tight,
I cry and bawl when I'm hungry at night,
When everyone's having their dinner, I sit in my bouncy chair,
They leave me there until they've finished, as if I don't care,
I adore my milk, so warm, so runny,
People pull silly faces at me, but I don't think they're funny,
I love playing with others, it's really very fun,
But when I need my nappy changed, everyone seems to run!

Emily Rogers (12)
Twynham School, Christchurch

Fairy Tale

A fairy tale is . . .

A doorway into another world,
Exciting,
A beautiful place,
Wonderful,
An enchanting journey,
A faraway adventure,
An amazing kingdom,
Fairies and goblins,
Big oak trees with wonders inside,
Glistening lakes,
Peaceful villages,
Refreshing waterfalls,
Green, lush grass,
Never-ending happiness,
Daydreams come true,
Witchcraft and cauldrons,
Spells and wishes.

Bethany De-Pledge (13)
Twynham School, Christchurch

Glide Into Night-Time

The bird was as soft as silk upon the water,
As gentle as a butterfly swooping through the reeds,
Whilst the sunset sat perched upon the horizon,
Glistening onto the lake like a mirror reflecting a silhouette.

Higher and higher the bird flew until it was a mere speck
Merging with the stars,
Following the bird as far as the eye could see,
It no longer looked like a bird, but like a freckle on the sky's face,
The stars formed a web, catching in the dark shadow
And the sunset faded away into the deep, deep night.

Emily Fardell (13)
Twynham School, Christchurch

My Generation

Listening to my MP3,
Instead of watching my TV,
Playing on my Game Boy,
Instead of painting a picture or playing with a toy,
This is my generation.

Texting on my mobile phone,
Instead of being on the beach, skimming stones,
Glued to my favourite DVD,
I should be playing outside until called in for tea,
This is my generation.

Power Point, Excel and Word,
Not a typewriter to be heard,
Doing my homework on the computer,
Is no longer a thing of the future,
This is my generation.

Hannah McGuigan (12)
Twynham School, Christchurch

The Decider

He's going toward the penalty spot,
The Argentinean skipper,
The gaffer is jumping and chewing his gum,
While the subs put their heads in their hands!

He'll be a legend in his country,
If he scores the deciding goal,
He knows that he's England's last chance,
To lift the 2010 World Cup!

Alex Burgess (11)
Twynham School, Christchurch

I'm To Blame

Heartbreaking,
Bootie shaking,
Mad hot,
Never stop,
Have a drink,
Don't think,
Have another,
Meet a guy,
Time passes by,
Drive the car,
Feeling sick,
Head thick,
Drank too much,
Massive crash,
Try to dash,
Covered in dirt,
People hurt,
Get caught,
Am distraught,
Behind bars,
Sealed in a room,
Life is over,
I'm to blame.

Annabel Heybourne (12)
Twynham School, Christchurch

Our Future

Wouldn't it be good if we all could see
That we are destroying our world to be?
For the rich and the poor
We are destroying the Earth's floor

If we change our power like me
We can have a better world to be
For the poor and the rich
We will stop our terrible glitch

The smoke and waste
Are dumped in haste
Which polluted our Earth
From its birth

Keep the grass and not the turf
As this is not the natural way of Earth
Keep our environment clean
Or the Earth will be mean

The waste has caused natural disasters
This could mean a shortage of plasters!
Disease has sprung its trap
So fast, you couldn't turn on the tap

We can stop the world from that
By thinking about wild cats
Animals and humans live on the same Earth
Let's not use fake turf.

Tobias Baril (11)
Twynham School, Christchurch

What Am I?

I stand here, watching, looking all around,
Seeing everything happen on the ground.
Children are playing and having fun,
But parents have to run, run, run!
Dogs are barking, wanting to play,
Everyone appears to be having such a lovely day.
Flowers come and flowers go,
It's a pleasure to watch things grow.
Every year, I get taller
And the things on the ground get smaller.
My colours change throughout the year,
But I will always remain right here.
Have you guessed what I could be?
Of course, I am a tree!

Jack Whitton (11)
Twynham School, Christchurch

My Poem

A dream is . . .

A world of your own
A way to imagine
A palace of the night
The kingdom of your mind
It's the door to another universe
The way to escape
A place to get lost

An endless darkness
A terrifying night
The scariest visions
Horrific flashbacks
They can make you jump out of your skin
Lasting forever . . .

Sophie Herbert (12)
Twynham School, Christchurch

Rugby In The Rain

The rain was falling on the ground like bombs
No one could stop and stand up
People were dropping the ball like a hot potato
Then I got the ball
I took it round people like a rocket

Then I scored
I dived on the ground
It felt like I was never going to stop
It was like a fairground ride
Then I stopped like a car crashing
Then I got up, I was so wet
I could fill a bath up with water

Rugby is my game
It's better in the rain!

Oliver Shortell (13)
Twynham School, Christchurch

The Wind

I was sitting, listening to the wind,
While trying to write this poem,
The gale outside was wild and whirling,
Almost like a hairdryer on full blast.

I could see the branches bending and buckling,
Stray leaves scatter, as the wind blows them about like toys
Litter going ferociously fast,
Tumbling and turning across the field.

Thoughts blew through my head,
I had to remember all those silly similes
And the awful alliteration and the rapid repetition,
Oh blow! This poem's going in the bin!

Emma Horn (12)
Twynham School, Christchurch

The Cat's Nap

The world is coming to an end,
But I don't give a whit, my friend.
I'll linger in a sunny spot,
Above the radiator hot;
I'll have a nap anyway.

The family left at half-past nine
And so the house is fully mine.
A shadow moved; must be alive,
Could jump up now, take a nose dive,
I'll have a nap anyway.

The dog, she interrupts my rest,
She is a giant, furry pest,
I need my beauty sleep just now,
Takes too much effort to *miaow*,
I'll have a nap anyway.

Something's fishy, but it's good,
There's tuna in the neighbourhood,
A tiny mouse is snoring fair;
He'll never know what hit him there,
I'll have a nap anyway.

My litter box emits a stench,
That makes my kitty teeth clench,
Perhaps I need to dig more sand,
To lend a feline helping hand,
I'll have a nap anyway.

Carla Tungate (12)
Twynham School, Christchurch

Abandoned

I've been left on my own,
In a dark and smelly street,
I want to be at home
And I can't feel my feet.

No one hears my cries,
I'm shaking with fear
And as time flies,
I know my owners aren't near.

I don't even have a bed;
I can't even get warm;
I just have dirt instead,
Who knows if there'll be a storm?

It's starting to rain,
I'm no longer dry,
But I still feel the same
And I start to cry.

Then a light comes from nowhere,
A figure comes to the door,
I stare, stare and stare,
I'm not alone anymore!

It's my nice, warm home,
My owners are here for me,
I'm no longer alone
And now I want my tea!

Emma Nunney (12)
Twynham School, Christchurch

Springtime Has Come At Last!

Springtime has come at last,
The sun is bright and gold!
Snowdrops have had their day,
As the daffodils unfold!

Birds busy making nests,
Flying out and about!
A tabby cat sneaks through the hedge,
Little fledglings, please watch out!

Baby lambs bleat in the field,
Staying close to Mother!
Be wary of a prowling fox,
Or any harmful other!

Cherry blossom, pink and pretty,
Twirling through the air!
Landing gently on a stream,
Gliding, with not a care!

Springtime has come at last!

Charlotte Hubbard (12)
Twynham School, Christchurch

My Garden In Summertime

The sun reflecting off the leaves,
A warm feeling of love,
The same songs from the birds in the trees.

A blackbird as white as a dove,
The sound of pure beauty when walking through the grass,
Warm but cold,
Sometimes sharper than glass.

When night falls, a full moon rises,
Bigger than ever,
Think of bigger surprises.

Day by day, can't wait till morning,
Relaxing and daydreaming,
Doodling and drawing.

The petals of the flowers,
Colours brighter than bright,
All closing up,
For a long sleep tonight.

Alexandra Wilson (13)
Twynham School, Christchurch

Stars

Celestial obscurity,
Celestial twilight,
Imagination is your own creation,
Dreams are envisioned . . .

The mystical layer,
Between then and forever,
Earth and outer space,
Has a certain interface.

The stars as a mark,
Of unending mass,
That sets us apart,
From the greatest creation.

The stars, shining like the sun,
But invisible at day,
Hence ends the universal flames,
Moan just as the wind does through time,
But always watch the stars shining by,
Watching you.

Hushai Ian Pineda (12)
Twynham School, Christchurch

Gentle Mother

I sit upon my nest up high in the tree,
Listening to the creaking bough and the rustling of the leaves,
I wait for my mate to bring me my food,
As I sit upon my precious brood,
My eggs wriggle, push and shove,
I wait for them to hatch and give their love,
Just when I thought I'd had enough,
They hatch into little balls of fluff,
They all are a month old now!
I watch them hop nervously along the creaking bough,
Waiting for that day to come,
When they too can fly and have some fun!

Hannah Brindley (12)
Twynham School, Christchurch

My Garden In Summertime

The sun reflecting off the leaves,
A warm feeling of love,
The same songs from the birds in the trees.

A blackbird as white as a dove,
The sound of pure beauty when walking through the grass,
Warm but cold,
Sometimes sharper than glass.

When night falls, a full moon rises,
Bigger than ever,
Think of bigger surprises.

Day by day, can't wait till morning,
Relaxing and daydreaming,
Doodling and drawing.

The petals of the flowers,
Colours brighter than bright,
All closing up,
For a long sleep tonight.

Alexandra Wilson (13)
Twynham School, Christchurch

Stars

Celestial obscurity,
Celestial twilight,
Imagination is your own creation,
Dreams are envisioned . . .

The mystical layer,
Between then and forever,
Earth and outer space,
Has a certain interface.

The stars as a mark,
Of unending mass,
That sets us apart,
From the greatest creation.

The stars, shining like the sun,
But invisible at day,
Hence ends the universal flames,
Moan just as the wind does through time,
But always watch the stars shining by,
Watching you.

Hushai Ian Pineda (12)
Twynham School, Christchurch

Gentle Mother

I sit upon my nest up high in the tree,
Listening to the creaking bough and the rustling of the leaves,
I wait for my mate to bring me my food,
As I sit upon my precious brood,
My eggs wriggle, push and shove,
I wait for them to hatch and give their love,
Just when I thought I'd had enough,
They hatch into little balls of fluff,
They all are a month old now!
I watch them hop nervously along the creaking bough,
Waiting for that day to come,
When they too can fly and have some fun!

Hannah Brindley (12)
Twynham School, Christchurch

A Book To Be Told

How many words do books behold?
Many words, but none to be told.
About fighters, princesses, dragons and more,
But none said about the book we adore.
Some books are thick, some books are thin,
Some books hold wisdom and courage.
Some don't hold anything,
Some are completely empty,
Waiting for you to pour into your pitiful whirlwind
Of your so-called life.
Some books want a home, a mini book, a wife,
My book sits on a dusty shelf
With no one, not a soul, just all by itself,
Waiting for someone so bold to say,
'I want this book, to take home today.'
He sighs and he sighs as he too has to hide
But nobody cares, only about the magic inside,
The book feels lonely now
And you may say, 'How?'
But only the book can tell you now
They only want to be read,
Grant them their wish,
Let them tell you their features,
Once you've read it, you won't need teachers!

Romy Garner (12)
Twynham School, Christchurch

Young Writers Information

We hope you have enjoyed reading this book - and that you will continue to enjoy it in the coming years.

If you like reading and writing poetry drop us a line, or give us a call, and we'll send you a free information pack.

Alternatively if you would like to order further copies of this book or any of our other titles, then please give us a call or log onto our website at www.youngwriters.co.uk

Young Writers Information
Remus House
Coltsfoot Drive
Peterborough
PE2 9JX
(01733) 890066